Y0-BUP-101

Piercing the
Veil of Secrecy

Piercing the
Veil of Secrecy

Litigation against U.S. Intelligence

Janine M. Brookner

CAROLINA ACADEMIC PRESS
Durham, North Carolina

ISBN 0-89089-221-0
LCCN 2003106101

Carolina Academic Press
700 Kent Street
Durham, NC 27701
Telephone (919) 489-7486
Fax (919) 493-5668
www.cap-press.com

Printed in the United States of America

DEDICATION

To:

my Colin—my long time ally and companion whose honesty, loyalty and intelligence I count on and who stands steadfastly by my side,

my Steven—my son, my friend, a visionary with integrity and imagination, who believes in me and a silver lining and gave me beautiful Caitlin (and later Brittany) to hold close to my heart while the world as I knew it came crashing down,

my Gary and my Arthur—my wonderful confreres, who help me find my smile and give me unconditional love, and

my Judy—my beautiful Judy, the wind beneath my wings.

CONTENTS

PART ONE
PROBLEMS, DEFENSES AND EXEMPTIONS

TABLE OF AUTHORITIES

Cases

Statutes

Other Authorities

Rules and Regulations

INTRODUCTION

If you are going to sin, sin against God, but not against the bureaucracy—
God will forgive you, the bureaucracy never will.
—Admiral Hyman Rickover

Behind a veil of secrecy and national security, United States intelligence agencies, particularly the Central Intelligence Agency (CIA or Agency), deprive thousands of current and former employees of important rights enjoyed by other American citizens. Required to sign a secrecy agreement as a condition of employment, for instance, all CIA employees understand when they enter on duty that, for the rest of their lives, their right to freedom of speech will be substantially curtailed.[1] They also understand that their right to foreign travel is contingent upon obtaining official permission and their privacy rights are surrendered because they must sign waivers permitting access to their credit, banking and other financial records.[2] What employees of intelligence agencies do not realize is that they face curtailment of another significant right, the right to seek relief under the Constitution and laws of the United States for illegal, discriminatory, and/or unfair employment actions.

---

1. Specifically, every CIA employee must agree to submit for review by the CIA "any writing or other preparation in any form, including a work of fiction, which contains any mention of intelligence data or activities," that the employee may even "contemplate disclosing publicly." CIA Secrecy Agreement, Form 305 (1991). The official purpose of this secrecy agreement is the protection of CIA sources and methods from unauthorized disclosure. *See* National Security Act of 1947, §103(c)(5), 50 U.S.C. §403-3(c)(5) (West Supp. 2001); the Central Intelligence Agency Act of 1949, §6, 50 U.S.C. §403(g) (West Supp. 2001); Exec. Order No. 12,333, §1.8(h), 46 Fed. Reg. 59,941 (Dec. 4, 1981); and DCID 1/14 (Apr. 14, 1986).

2. Intelligence Authorization Act for Fiscal Year 1995, Pub. L. No. 103-359, §801(a)(3), (4) (codified, as amendment of the National Security Act of 1947 by adding Title VIII— Access to Classified Information, 50 U.S.C.A. §435a(3), (4) (West 2000)).

On paper, intelligence agencies have equitable rules and regulations that purport to offer protection to their employees against unlawful or prejudicial practices. In reality, however, these rules often are ignored by senior management, applied selectively to the rank and file to suppress dissent and whistle-blowing or used to circumvent federal law.[3] Moreover, internal regulations clearly fail when knowledge of how the system works and the probability of being tainted and harmed professionally prevents even sympathetic employees from assisting an aggrieved colleague. If the employee then turns to the judicial system, normal rules applicable to civil actions are overridden in the name of national security, even when, in fact, national security is not threatened and the true objective is to cover up wrongdoing and to prevent employees from seeking redress of their grievances.

This book discusses actual CIA cases, demonstrating and explaining through these cases the unique problems plaintiffs and their counsel face when attempting to sue U.S. intelligence agencies. Initially, it explores methods which the CIA uses to exert control over the legal process. These include: restricting an employee's choice and number of lawyers; abusing the redaction process; misusing security and secrecy to deny access to information, evidence and witnesses, and regulating attorneys' actions on behalf of clients through the exploitation and manipulation of the secrecy agreement which lawyers are forced to sign.

From the beginning of a case against the CIA, for example, both the complainant and counsel are led to believe that if a lawyer obtains a CIA security clearance and signs a secrecy agreement, the attorney will be given access to information and evidence needed to pursue a possible legal action. In reality, however, when the Agency grants a clearance to opposing counsel, the lawyer becomes bound by a secrecy agreement that disadvantages the client. The CIA exploits the security clearance to control and intimidate a complainant's legal representative and to gain access to privileged attorney-client material and the plaintiff's evidence and information. Worse still, signing the secrecy agreement forces counsel to submit to the CIA for redaction all documentation prior to filing any material in court, giving the CIA the prerogative to eliminate adverse or embarrassing information by falsely claiming it is classified. In return, the lawyer receives nothing from the CIA. Despite the clearance, the CIA generally denies opposing counsel access to each and every piece of

---

3. Agency Regulation (AR) 9-2 is an example of a CIA internal regulation which purports to set out procedures to handle sexual and hostile work environment harassment at the CIA. In actuality, AR 9-2 establishes a mechanism to circumvent the protections to which an employee is entitled pursuant to Title VII of the Civil Rights Act of 1964.

information he or she requests and needs, even unclassified regulations and policies.

In addition, U.S. government agencies, and particularly the CIA, obstruct and delay the internal processing of cases, legal proceedings, and the payment of settlement awards and legal costs and fees. This relentless obstruction of justice inflicts further harm on the plaintiff professionally, emotionally and financially.

Moreover, the CIA places other impediments in the path of the employee who attempts to redress a grievance. Managers within the Offices of the Inspector General, Medical Services, Equal Employment Opportunity, the General Counsel and Security, who have the responsibility and power to rectify a bad situation, instead, may exacerbate it by colluding and conspiring to close all avenues of relief. Retaliation and reprisal against the complainant often become commonplace. Then to quash the spread of information about such practices, secrecy and the need to protect cover are used to cover up and prevent aggrieved Agency officers from speaking out.

Worse still for the already disadvantaged plaintiff is the CIA's relationship with certain judges. According to a former CIA attorney, the Agency sends its lawyers out to brief judges, ex parte, on cases pending before the court. Reportedly, there is close and continuing contact between CIA lawyers and some district court judges, even when the CIA is the defendant.

Chapters Two and Three of this book turn to the issues of sovereign immunity and the CIA as an exempted Agency. The CIA's exclusion from federal laws which provide protection to most U.S. government employees under the Civil Service Reform Act[4] and the Whistleblower Protection Act[5] is herein addressed.

With all these exclusions and exceptions as well as the obstructive maneuvers that the U.S. intelligence agencies, particularly the CIA, use to control the legal process and punish the plaintiff, the question arises: Is it actually possible to successfully sue an intelligence agency? The main thrust of this book attempts to answer this question and explore feasible legal avenues that could be exploited by government employees and their attorneys in civil actions against U.S. intelligence.

Title VII, which governs equal employment opportunity matters, is enforceable against all U.S. government agencies, including the CIA, and, there-

---

4. Civil Service Reform Act of 1978 (CSRA), Pub. L. No. 95-454, 92 Stat. 1111 (codified as amended in scattered sections of 5 U.S.C.).

5. Whistleblower Protection Act of 1989 (WPA), Pub. L. No. 101-12, §3(i), 103 Stat. 16; 5 U.S.C. §1201 (West 1996).

fore, available in discrimination cases for those in specific federally-protected categories such as women and certain minorities.[6] An employee in one of these categories who believes he or she is the target of discrimination must first exhaust all internal administrative remedies before pursuing the case in district court or through the Equal Employment Opportunity Commission (EEOC). A CIA complainant can expect this internal processing to take well over two years, rather than the circa one year allowed by EEOC-mandated deadlines.[7] In a Title VII suit against the government, only the head of agency in his official capacity is a proper party defendant. Other managers in their official or individual capacities cannot be named as defendants, no matter how egregious their behavior. An important discussion in this section focuses on whether Title VII is a plaintiff's exclusive remedy for injuries suffered due to unlawful employment discrimination and/or other adverse personnel actions, precluding other federal statutory and constitutional claims.

Under the Federal Tort Claims Act (FTCA), legal action against the U.S. government may be taken for select causes of action such as negligent hiring and supervision and the infliction of emotional distress. The federal government cannot be held liable for the torts of libel or slander unless it waives its immunity, clearly a most unlikely prospect and not one to be expected particularly when suing intelligence agencies.[8] Requirements under the FTCA include: first exhausting administrative remedies; filing an administrative claim for a sum certain before filing a suit in court; suing the U.S. government, not particular agencies or individuals in either their official or personal capacities, and observing a two-year statue of limitations.

After discussing Title VII and the FTCA, where Congress clearly waived the government's sovereign immunity for certain conduct, this book delves further, researching how and under what other bases may an aggrieved party sue individual intelligence officials. An analysis follows which indicates that the precedent setting case of *Bivens* indeed may provide the legal basis for litigation against U.S. intelligence actors for constitutional violations of an employee's rights. The Supreme Court in *Bivens* held that the deprivation of a constitutional guarantee by a federal agent acting under the color of law gives rise to a cause of action for damages, as long as a named individual federal

---

6. Title VII of the Civil Rights Act of 1964, 42 U.S.C. §2000e-16(c) (West 1997); *see also* 29 C.F.R. §§1614.402, 1614.403, 1614.408 (implementing regulations) (1999).

7. *See* EEOC Management Directive (EEO MD-110).

8. Under the Federal Tort Claims Act of 1946 (FTCA), 28 U.S.C.A. sections 2674 and 2680(h) (West 1994), "The United States shall be liable, respecting the provisions of this title relating to tort claims…Exceptions…(h) any claim arising out of…libel, slander.…"

defendant knew or reasonably should have known that his act would violate the plaintiff's constitutional right.[9] The personal injury statute of limitation in the state where the *Bivens* claim is filed usually provides the applicable time limit for such cases, whether or not the action is brought in district or state court. Case precedent demonstrates that a *Bivens* action may lie even where other remedies are available.

A subsequent Chapter looks at the very real feasibility of a suit against U.S. intelligence officials for employment-related civil rights conspiracies under 42 U.S.C.§§1985 and 1986. It addresses three areas: conspiracy to interfere with the performance of official duties by a federal officer;[10] conspiracy to obstruct justice,[11] and conspiracy to deprive a person of equal protection and equal privileges and immunities.[12] Section 1986 provides a damage remedy against anyone who knew that the wrongs conspired to be done were about to be committed, had the power to prevent or aid in preventing them and neglected or refused to do so.

A discussion of the concept of pursuing a civil RICO action against colluding U.S. intelligence agency employees follows. The elements of the claim are that the conspirators committed two or more predicate acts in connection with the conduct of an enterprise which injured another employee in his or her business or property.[13] Given the possibility of triple damages and the payment of attorney fees, civil RICO may be a particularly attractive claim for a plaintiff to make against intelligence officials under the right circumstances. To date, however, RICO has not been pursued successfully against the CIA.

This book ends by suggesting administrative and procedural changes which could alleviate some of the problems and abuses that an employee of an intelligence agency faces when suing his or her employer. Merely requiring U.S. intelligence agencies to comply with the some of the Federal Rules of Civil Procedure would assist substantially in leveling the playing field between the litigant and the government.

Although the focus here is on legal actions against U.S. intelligence agencies, particularly the CIA, the analyses, problems and possible solutions are applicable in civil suits against other U.S. governmental entities which misuse secrecy and national security to thwart the legitimate rights of employees.

---

9. *Bivens v. Six Unknown Fed. Narcotics Agents*, 403 U.S. 388, 390 (1971).

10. 42 U.S.C. § 1985(1) (West 1994).

11. 42 U.S.C. § 1985(2) (West 1994).

12. 42 U.S.C. § 1985(3) (West 1994).

13. Civil Racketeer Influenced and Corrupt Organizations Act (RICO), 18 U.S.C. §§1961, 1962, 1964 (West 2000).

Counselors for plaintiffs in employment-related legal actions, who are up against seemingly formidable opponents such as the Federal Bureau of Investigation, the National Security Agency, parts of the Department of State, the Department of Defense, the Department of Energy and the Drug Enforcement Agency, as well as their Department of Justice lawyers, will find this book has good practical utility for them. Those suing or contemplating suing U.S. Intelligence need to know beforehand what they are up against, what to expect, the intimidation tactics they will face and how best to pursue a legal action. Judges, senators and members of congress also should be aware when deciding cases or making laws of just how unlevel and unfair the playing field actually is when plaintiffs sue the CIA and other agencies that hide behind the veil of secrecy. In addition, this book should be useful as a textbook and educational tool for students, professors of law and law groups interested in national security, civil rights and employment rights.

Actual CIA Cases

This section describes actual CIA cases that are used for illustrative purposes in this book. A CIA complainant in the Directorate of Operations (DO), also known as the Clandestine Service, is required by the CIA to select an alias before seeking the advice of counsel. Where there is a known CIA-assigned alias, it is used below. If the complainant's Agency alias is unknown or where the CIA has forced the plaintiff to agree to a "gag order" as a condition of a settlement, a pseudonym is used to protect the concerned party. A true name, therefore, is provided here in only one case in which the complainant was an overt Agency employee, meaning she worked for the CIA but not under cover. The case descriptions themselves are accurate.

A. *Ellis v. Tenet*, Director, Central Intelligence Agency, No. 90-03, Appeal No. 01940566, Hearing No. 033-92-2014X, EEOC, 24 October 1995; CA-98-1058-A (E.D. Va. Sept. 11, 1998); No. 98-2481, (4th Cir. 10 Sept. 1999). Ellis (true name), a senior officer in the CIA's Office of Medical Services (OMS), enjoyed a successful, rewarding and lengthy career with the CIA. Her achievements, however, were marred by her long-term involvement with her supervisor, a married doctor. Ellis' efforts to sever the relationship resulted in retaliation by this supervisor, including his refusal to keynote the hostage-rescue and anti-terrorism courses which she coordinated or to allow her to travel overseas on work-related temporary assignments. The supervisor stalked her, purchasing an apartment adjacent to hers to watch her comings and goings. When Ellis finally and permanently terminated her relationship with the supervisor, her career ended as well. Ellis began receiving marginal evaluations. She was ranked in the lowest ten percentile of her peer group. Her OMS position was eliminated and she was given the choice to retire or be declared excess and fired.

Ellis initially filed a gender discrimination complaint with the CIA's Office of Equal Employment Opportunity (OEEO) in 1987. Her first lawyer, one on the list of "cleared" attorneys which the CIA's Office of General Counsel (OGC) used to provide Agency employees, proved to be unsatisfactory. Ellis' subsequent attorney did not want to pursue her case in the conservative and reputedly pro-CIA District Court for the Eastern District of Virginia. Rather, he chose the Equal Employment Opportunity Commission (EEOC) route. When the EEOC administrative judge decided in Ellis' favor, the CIA ignored the ruling, asked for reconsideration or appealed. This tactic enabled the CIA to prolong the case for years.

Finally, Ellis decided to retain an attorney to file her case in federal court. Unfortunately, Title VII of the Civil Rights Act of 1964, 42 U.S.C. § 2000e-5(f)(3)(West 1994), specifies that venue lies in the judicial district where the unlawful employment practice is alleged to have occurred, where the relevant employment records are maintained, or where the aggrieved person would have worked but for the alleged unlawful employment practice. Hence, the Agency succeeded in transferring Ellis' case to the District Court for the Eastern District of Virginia. The CIA then refused to allow either Ellis or her new Agency-cleared attorney access to Ellis' documentation that the CIA required her to store in a safe at a CIA facility. The Agency unilaterally decided that neither Ellis nor her lawyer needed to see this information, because it was "irrelevant." Ellis' counsel, consequently, had to argue in federal court against the CIA's motion to dismiss her case without the benefit of the evidence which his client had earmarked for possible litigation. Moreover, the district court judge dismissed the case, refusing to allow Ellis' attorney leave to amend her complaint, even though the CIA had not served a responsive pleading.

B. *Betty* and her spouse worked for the CIA as a tandem couple. While they were posted in an East Asian country, she reported her husband to CIA station management for assaulting and beating her. One such violent incident occurred on the premises of a United States government facility in the presence of other Americans. Instead of faulting the husband, the CIA took action against Betty, characterizing her behavior as disruptive. The CIA's OMS then conducted an indirect psychological assessment of Betty without her knowledge. As a result of that assessment, OMS placed a medical hold on Betty. This hold prevented her from obtaining an overseas assignment, thereby harming her chances for career advancement. She filed a discrimination complaint, requesting that the medical hold be removed, that she be given a posting abroad, and that her attorney fees be paid. After switching from an attorney on OGC's "cleared" list to more forceful counsel, Betty prevailed. Betty was required to agree to a gag order as a condition of settlement.

C. *Thompson v. Woolsey, Director of the Central Intelligence Agency, et al.,* No. 94-923-A (E.D. Va. 14 July 1994, amended 6 September 1994 and 25 October 1994). Thompson, the first female CIA Chief of Station (COS) in Latin America, sued the CIA and individual Agency defendants for violating her constitutional rights, conspiracy and sex discrimination. Her problems with the Agency began when she reported her deputy for the repeated and admitted battering of his wife. The deputy, angered that Thompson blew the whistle on him, duped the CIA's Office of the Inspector General (OIG) which investigated Thompson rather than the deputy. Thompson's formerly exceptional professional career came to an abrupt standstill, and her promised second overseas COS assignment disappeared. Thompson was easily able to disprove fact-based allegations, but then the OIG, refusing to admit it had made a mistake, attacked her character, accusing her of wearing "imperceptible" underwear and sexually harassing a male subordinate. The OIG refused to indicate when and where this conduct ostensibly occurred or identify any witnesses, including the alleged male subordinate, and totally ignored Thompson's evidence and affidavits. It was only after Thompson filed a civil action in federal court that she and her lawyers were given enough information to demonstrate that the OIG and/or its informants (Thompson's male deputy and his cohorts) had fabricated evidence. The so-called subordinate whom Thompson had sexually harassed turned out to be the head of the Drug Enforcement Agency (DEA) in the Latin American country where Thompson and the DEA official were posted. The DEA official submitted a sworn affidavit verifying that no such harassment had taken place and that no one from the CIA's OIG or the Department of Justice (DOJ), which represented the CIA, had ever even spoken to him. The same day that Thompson's lawyers presented this affidavit to DOJ lawyers, they agreed to give Thompson a handsome settlement and separately pay her legal bills. In their rush to settle after the CIA was caught in this lie, the DOJ attorneys forgot to place a "gag order" on the settlement. Consequently, when Thompson chose to retire, the CIA, in an effort to keep her quiet about Agency wrongdoing, tried to force her to remain under the official cover of another U.S. government agency rather than admit she had been a long-time CIA officer. This attempt to gag Thompson proved farcical in the face of the large amount of publicity that her case already had generated.

D. A *class action* was filed as *Conway v. Deutch, Director of the Central Intelligence Agency*, No. 95-426-A (E.D. Va. June 9, 1995). The class was composed of women operations officers in the CIA's Clandestine Service who claimed they were discriminated against on the basis of gender. After two years, this action was settled—a handful of women were given promotions, many more received small cash payments and the attorneys were paid. Additionally, the court committed itself to oversee the progress of women in operations for a limited period of time. Nine of the ten women class agents opposed this pro-CIA settlement as inadequate, but the federal judge in the

Eastern District of Virginia District Court decided at a fairness hearing to force acceptance of the settlement upon the women.

E. *Doris*, a foreign-born woman of color over age forty, had a consistently excellent CIA career, received cash awards for superior performance and was nominated for CIA secretary of the year. While she was posted in an East Asian country, she had reason to file a discrimination complaint and report a possible security incident. The discrimination complaint was never investigated by the CIA, as required by federal law pursuant to Title VII. Nonetheless, subsequent to her complaint, the CIA's OMS performed an indirect psychological assessment of her without her knowledge or participation. Unbeknownst to Doris, a medical hold then was placed on her. At the same time, the OIG turned Doris's complaint against her, making Doris the target of an investigation. When she finally read a copy of the OIG report and explained to the OIG why it was erroneous, the OIG took the report and Doris' notes from her and refused to give her or her attorney access to the final OIG report. Meanwhile, Doris filed another discrimination complaint. As an apparent result of her complaints, she was denied scores of assignments both at CIA headquarters and abroad for which she was qualified and had applied. For well over a year she sat isolated at CIA headquarters with no substantive job. She was reduced to the humiliating position of going from office to office asking for work. After unsuccessfully trying to give a message to the CIA's Director, George Tenet, about the Agency's maltreatment of her and then appealing to her Congressman and Senator for redress of her grievances, Doris was placed on administrative leave and then terminated by Tenet. As with *Betty*, case B above, the CIA characterized Doris's behavior as disruptive.

F. *M.K.*, a veteran CIA employee with more than 25 years of service, was on a temporary assignment abroad when 25 CIA laptop computers, still containing top secret information on their hard-drives, were sold in Washington, D.C. at public auction. This major security lapse went undetected until months later when an individual who had purchased a number of the computers discovered some of the classified files. Despite an intensive search by the Federal Bureau of Investigation, several computers have never been recovered. An internal investigation faulted M.K. although she had no responsibility for the computers in question. M.K. was used as a scapegoat and given a reprimand.

M.K. retained a lawyer, but the CIA's OGC refused to allow M.K.'s CIA-cleared attorney to examine any of the documents, policies, procedures or regulations relevant to her case. Further, OGC even refused to show the attorney CIA regulations governing what client-related documentation he could and could not review. In September 1998, the CIA issued a policy notice entitled

"Access to Agency Facilities, Information, and Personnel by Private Counsel and Other Personal Representatives." This policy notice prohibited CIA employees from providing documents containing "official information" to their cleared counsel without OGC authorization. Official information was defined in the policy notice as "all information, whether classified or unclassified, that is originated, received or controlled by the...CIA...."[1] The CIA, in effect, interposed itself into the attorney-client relationship and denied M.K.'s counsel access to the information he needed to pursue her case.

G. *Evelyn Conway* alleged discrimination as a continuing violation based on her national origin and retaliation. Conway, a native speaker of a Slavic language, was born in an Eastern European country. She became a naturalized U.S. citizen at age 20. Conway's Eastern European background, language capability, and masters degree in business administration were precisely the reasons the CIA hired her, and yet her ethnic origin was precisely the reason the CIA did not trust her. As a result, for years the CIA refused to give her career-enhancing assignment opportunities, forbade her to work in any area related to Eastern Europe and forced her out of the operational career track of the Clandestine Service.

In trying to pursue her case and meet the requirement to exhaust all internal administrative avenues of possible relief before filing in court, Conway encountered numerous obstacles and delays in which the CIA blatantly violated her constitutional right to procedural due process. The CIA denied and obstructed her counsel, ignored mandated deadlines,[2] altered the issues and bases of her complaints without her agreement, rejected her legitimate allegations and circumvented Title VII requirements by transferring the handling of her case out of the CIA's OEEO.

H. *Hannah* was told by her CIA manager that she was too attractive and strong-willed to be posted to a particular African country. Knowing that a man would never be denied a foreign assignment on those bases, Hannah reported this gender discrimination to the CIA's OEEO. As a result, she, not the manager, was investigated by the OIG, which attempted to intimidate her with charges of wrongfully obtaining a visa for a friend. Although the CIA manager denied making any comment about Hannah's attractiveness and strong will, a CIA OEEO counselor admitted during a deposition that the manager had confessed to her that he indeed had made the statement. Immediately after the manager was caught in this lie, the CIA agreed to settle by paying Hannah compensatory damages, removing all derogatory information from her file,

---

1. *See* Second Amended Complaint, *Class Action, M.K. v. Tenet*, CA 1:99CV95(RMU) (*M.K. I*) at 4–17.

2. Pursuant to 29 C.F.R. § 1614 (2000) and EEOC Management Directive (EEO MD-110).

giving her an assignment abroad, and paying her legal fees. Despite the agreement, the CIA delayed finalizing and signing the settlement for nearly a year. As a condition of settlement, Hannah had to agree to a "gag order."

I. *Ira*, a male COS in a European country used his special communication channel with the Director of Central Intelligence (DCI) to report alleged illegal activity by the CIA's OIG. Ira requested that the DCI inform the House and Senate Intelligence Oversight Committees regarding this misconduct. Instead, the DCI's attorney showed the communication to the CIA's Inspector General himself. Ira's promised future assignment disappeared, and he was transferred to an out-of-the way CIA facility in Virginia, where he had little or no responsibility or work. Realizing he had virtually no future in the CIA, Ira retired.

J. *Jill*, a female Clandestine Service officer married to another Agency employee, was the subject of an attempted rape by a CIA officer while on a temporary assignment to a European station. When she resisted, the would-be rapist beat her. Upon returning to CIA headquarters, Jill and her husband reported the assault and attempted rape to the CIA's OEEO. The OEEO Director told them to forgive and forget. The couple demanded the CIA report the matter to the DOJ for possible criminal prosecution. Although the assailant admitted the attempted rape, the OIG's investigative report blamed the female victim. Jill, an excellent linguist and operations officer, was relegated to clerical work. Her husband, a scientist, was forced to load trucks and perform logistical support work for the CIA. The couple sued, and the day before their pleading was to be filed in federal district court, the CIA settled under terms satisfactory to Jill and her spouse. They were forced to agree to be gagged regarding the settlement. Both talented young CIA officers immediately resigned.

K. *Katherine*—not a CIA staff employee but the abused wife of an Agency officer—was forced by the CIA to undergo a psychiatric evaluation after reporting to the COS in the Latin American country where she and her husband were posted that her husband had beaten her three times. The second report of physical abuse came after the COS asked Katherine, a native Spanish speaker, to participate in a risky clandestine operation which required language expertise but for which she had no training. She declined, which angered the COS, who punished Katherine's husband by removing him from the operation. The husband retaliated, brutally beating his wife and breaking furniture over her body after he tied a scarf around her mouth to muffle her screams. The distraught wife, appealing for assistance, went to the COS' office the following day and showed him her bruised face, shoulders and arms. The COS smiled and commented, "Now we're even," referring to her refusal to participate in the clandestine operation. The COS then further humiliated Katherine by sending a message through Department of State (DOS) channels, that Katherine (not the husband) was required to see an OMS psychiatrist to determine her suitability to remain abroad.[3] This unclassified cable received wide distribution in the Embassy and CIA headquarters, as well as the DOS.

L. *Lilah*, a member of the CIA class action composed of female operations officers, was accused of drunkenness and lesbianism when she disagreed with her CIA boss while stationed in Europe.[4] According to Lilah, neither allegation was true. Nevertheless, as a result, she was sent to another overseas station where she was required to undergo tests for alcoholism.

M. *MaryAnn*, a CIA secretary, for years has battled allegations by the CIA's Office of Security that she is a lesbian. Although she vehemently denied these accusations and no evidence of lesbianism was ever presented, these accusations continued to haunt her with every attempt to successfully complete the required five-year re-investigation polygraph and obtain the Office of Security's approval to work overseas. Although the Agency is no longer permitted to discriminate and fire its employees on the basis of sexual orientation, it remains a homophobic organization that still views homosexuals as security risk.

---

3. The COS was rewarded for his excellent work in Latin America Division. He continued on to assume two of the CIA's best COS positions in Europe.

4. The CIA claims it no longer discriminates against homosexuals.

PART ONE

PROBLEMS, DEFENSES AND EXEMPTIONS

The first chapters of this book attempt to provide lawyers and plaintiffs with an understanding of what they will encounter when suing an intelligence agency, particularly the CIA. The defenses of absolute immunity and qualified immunity then are considered, followed by a discussion of what cannot be done and what statutes are not applicable because of exemptions and exclusions. These chapters should help prepare attorneys and aggrieved parties for the difficult problems involved in litigation against U.S. intelligence.

CHAPTER ONE

UNIQUE PROBLEMS EMPLOYEES ENCOUNTER WHEN SUING UNITED STATES INTELLIGENCE

As difficult as it may be for any individual to sue his or her employer, those working for U.S. intelligence agencies face a variety of additional obstacles not normally found in the outside world. Most of these problems stem from the misuse or abuse of security to control the aggrieved employee and opposing counsel's information, evidence and witnesses. Intelligence agencies also manipulate legal procedures and regulations, continually obstructing and delaying the progress of cases, sometimes in violation of federal statutes and rules. Moreover, the complainant is subjected to intimidation, collusion, retaliation and reprisals. These problems increase the emotional and financial costs of litigation and may force victims to give up in the face of what the government wants its opposition to believe are insurmountable odds. The worst of the offenders appears to be the CIA.

A. Methods Used by CIA to Exert Control over Legal Process

1. Restricting Employee's Choice of Counsel

Imagine a defendant being allowed to play a key role in selecting the lawyer who will represent his opponent in a legal proceeding. That is exactly what happens when a CIA employee attempts to retain an attorney to litigate against the Agency.

From the moment Agency complainants decide to avail themselves of possible judicial remedies, they are confronted with the CIA's exploitation of security in an effort to exert control over the entire legal process, including their choice of counsel. As a first step in any possible action against the CIA, employees generally meet with an officer in the Agency's Office of General Counsel (OGC). During these early stages, unsuspecting complainants seldom realize that OGC's function is to protect the Agency, not its employees. When employees express a desire to consult an attorney, they are warned against even speaking to one who does not hold a CIA security clearance. OGC maintains a list of "cleared" lawyers, from which employees have been expected to select counsel. More and more CIA employees, however, are learning to avoid attorneys on the list, and OGC, after receiving adverse publicity about its "cleared" lawyers list, is not immediately offering it to Agency complainants.

Being on the CIA's list of cleared attorneys creates a potential conflict of interest for lawyers. It gives an attorney an opening to a new client base, but may jeopardize the lawyer's willingness to litigate zealously against the Agency. At least two women pursuing Title VII employment discrimination cases determined that their CIA-recommended representatives were unwilling or unable to doggedly battle the seemingly formidable CIA.[1] After wasting a good deal of time and money, both women hired other lawyers, not on OGC's already "cleared" list, who tried to pick up the pieces and bring their cases to more palatable resolutions.

If an Agency employee selects his or her own representative, not one on OGC's list, the CIA insists that it must grant a security clearance to that attorney before the employee is allowed to meet the lawyer. A Clandestine Service officer, in fact, is not even permitted to speak with his or her lawyer of choice, nor provide his or her true name or Agency affiliation, until the attorney is cleared by the CIA. This restriction, if followed, means that no covert CIA employee may discuss with an uncleared attorney any work-related dispute, even one which involves no secret issues, such as straight employment discrimination.

In reality, legal representation of an Agency employee generally does not require the complainant's lawyer to have a CIA security clearance. An attorney can pursue most adverse personnel cases against the CIA without having access to classified information. Aliases can be and are used in litigation and specific locations of CIA stations do not have to be mentioned in court documentation.

Even after granting a CIA clearance to a plaintiff's attorney, there still may be some question whether an Agency employee is allowed to speak to the lawyer. When CIA management invited female operations officers who were

---

1. *Ellis*, case A and *Betty*, case B.

actual or potential members of an ongoing class action to attend a meeting, the Agency's General Counsel was asked by one class member whether she was permitted to speak with the cleared attorneys representing the class. The General Counsel told her that she might be able to do so, but only at her own peril.[2] This answer left the class member confused and fearful, which obviously was the CIA's objective.

Although the CIA's clearance process for a complainant's lawyer involves only a name trace and the OGC is able to provide a security clearance in less than 24 hours, it advises the employee that it takes up to six weeks or more to complete the clearance process. In the meantime, these delays in granting clearances to opposing counsel may cause the employee, who is not well versed in the law, to lose his or her right to file a complaint on the grounds of untimeliness. An individual who believes he or she was the subject of discrimination, for example, may be precluded from initiating a complaint with the CIA's Office of Equal Employment Opportunity (OEEO) if that employee is waiting for an attorney to be cleared and not aware that the deadline for meeting with an OEEO counselor to report discrimination is 45 days from the day of the alleged act or the day he or she knew or reasonably should have known of the discrimination.[3]

Although EEOC guidelines allow for the postponement of the pre-complaint counseling stage until the aggrieved party's representative is cleared, the CIA has refused complainants' legitimate requests for such postponements. One aggrieved party's attorney, for example, was not cleared by the CIA to represent her until the day the pre-complaint counseling stage ended.[4] As a result, she was denied legal representation during the entire pre-complaint counseling period, in violation of federal rules and procedures.[5] Moreover, two CIA OEEO officers wrongfully advised the complainant that she did not need an attorney during this stage and that hiring a lawyer would be a waste of her money. Consequently, the aggrieved employee was forced to prepare the issues and bases of her discrimination claims without benefit of counsel. The

2. *Class action*, case D. Although the right to counsel is guaranteed by Amendment VI of the Constitution only in criminal prosecutions, Amendment V, which provides that no person shall "be deprived of life or property, without due process of law," arguably may provide a parallel right in civil cases.

3. *See* 29 C.F.R. § 1614 (2000) and the EEOC Management Directive (EEO MD-110), for time and procedural guidelines.

4. *Conway*, case G.

5. The denial of counsel violates 29 C.F.R. § 1614.605 (2000) and EEO MD-110.

same OEEO officer, who earlier had advised complainant that hiring counsel was a waste of money, then dismissed the issues and bases of discrimination that the complainant had identified.

Another tactic of the CIA is to revoke the security clearance it already has granted to a lawyer. The CIA's security guidelines for discrimination cases, dated September 18, 1998, states:

> *The Agency reserves the right to withdraw your representative's security clearance at any time* for just cause, such as receiving information indicating your representative has breached the terms of his or her secrecy/nondisclosure agreement or the obligations specified by OGC in a letter to your representative or *learning any other information* that indicates your representative cannot have continued access to classified information (emphasis added).[6]

Apparently "just cause" for revoking a lawyer's clearance can be that the attorney was too zealous or successful an advocate for his or her CIA client. In the *Thompson* case, the CIA canceled her lawyer's security clearance after Thompson prevailed.[7] Although the CIA need not, and generally does not, provide any reason to attorneys for canceling their security clearance, Thompson's lawyer finally learned that the Agency's pretext for the revocation was that she had used an uncleared employee of the firm to file Thompson's court papers.

Moreover, the CIA never informed Thompson's lawyer that it had rescinded her clearance. She only learned of it when other potential CIA clients tried to retain her but were told by the CIA's OGC to look elsewhere for counsel since she was no longer cleared.

CIA security policies regarding opposing counsel clearly are arbitrary. They give the CIA the opportunity to deny a complainant the right to an attorney at whim, without providing any reason or justification for its actions.

2. Restricting Employee's Number of Attorneys

By controlling the clearance process for attorneys, the CIA attempts to control not only an aggrieved party's right to select a lawyer of his or her choice, but also how many people in a law firm may work on a specific case. The CIA

---

6. U.S. Equal Employment Opportunity Comm'n, Security Guidelines for EEO Complaints 1 (1998).

7. *Thompson*, case C.

decides when the other side has enough lawyers, paralegals, and secretaries, and it will refuse to clear any more. In recent cases, in fact, the CIA has refused to clear more than a single attorney per complainant, while the CIA's OGC employs over 100 full-time lawyers, with as many as six to eight of them working against that same aggrieved individual. Additionally, when plaintiffs file their suits in court, the CIA's legal staff is augmented by DOJ lawyers. This CIA tactic of limiting the number of cleared law firm personnel serves two functions: (a) it keeps an outnumbered, lone opposing attorney overworked and often tied up in bureaucratic red tape, and (b) it forces the complainant to pay high legal fees for work that junior lawyers, paralegals or clericals could and should perform. In response to Thompson's lawyers' request for the CIA regulations regarding the number of cleared attorneys the Agency allows for any given plaintiff, an OGC lawyer admitted that no such regulation existed.[8]

When the lawyers in the *Thompson* case found themselves having to perform research and clerical work that could be accomplished by other law firm employees for much less than the $250 to $300 per hour they charged, they requested Agency security clearances for two additional members of the firm, a junior attorney and a secretary. The CIA refused, claiming that enough people were cleared for the case.

In addition, the CIA claims its security clearance for a lawyer representing an employee is case specific. When Thompson's lawyers asked to show her draft pleading to an attorney with expertise in civil rights who had already been cleared for the CIA women's class action case, the Agency claimed that the civil rights attorney was cleared only for the class action and was not permitted to read Thompson's draft.[9]

Another complainant received similar answers and treatment when she requested CIA security clearances on two lawyers for her Title VII discrimination complaint.[10] She was advised by a CIA OEEO counselor that OEEO's Chief of Complaints determined that only one lawyer would be cleared because CIA policy was one lawyer per complainant. When she requested a copy of the CIA's written policy limiting the aggrieved person to only one attorney, she was told that the policy was unwritten but that two CIA offices, OEEO and OGC, together had decided that she did not need to have another representative.

The women's class action lawyers encountered the same treatment when they asked the Agency to clear additional attorneys.[11] Moreover, when the large

---

8. *Thompson,* case C.
9. *Class action,* case D.
10. *Conway,* case G.
11. *Class Action,* case D.

majority of female class agents found themselves dissatisfied with their legal representation and tried to hire another lawyer, the CIA refused to clear him. This other lawyer, by coincidence, was a former (fully cleared) CIA officer who had never had any security blemishes during his Agency career.

The CIA's unilateral, unwritten policy limiting an employee's right to choose his or her own legal representation enables the CIA as a defendant to allot to itself the authority to select who a plaintiff's lawyer(s) will be, when and if the lawyer(s) will be cleared and how many legal representatives a plaintiff is allowed. This initial manipulation of complainants and attorneys, however, is only the tip of the iceberg in the CIA's attempts to control a complainant's case.

3. Exploitation of Lawyer's Secrecy Agreement

Since the CIA's authority to protect the security of its activities and information "by appropriate means" extends not only to its employees and contractors, but also to "other persons with similar association with the CIA as are necessary,"[12] the CIA insists attorneys who represent Agency employees sign a secrecy agreement. The CIA extends this practice even to lawyers for employees' spouses or relatives who have no direct dealings with the CIA or security matters. For example, the CIA demanded that the lawyers for a reportedly abused woman suing her CIA spouse for divorce sign a secrecy agreement.[13] Neither the wife nor her attorneys had ever worked for the CIA or had access to any classified information.

The CIA, in fact, exploits the security clearance to control opposing counsel, attorney-client information, and court documentation. The CIA Secrecy/Nondisclosure Agreement (form 305, 1991) which the Agency requires a complainant's CIA-cleared lawyer to sign forces counsel to yield to the CIA all complaints, motions and briefs before filing them in court and to agree never to publish "either by work, conduct, or any other means, such information" without specific authorization to do so by the CIA. Those lawyers who sign the agreement obligate themselves to first submit to the CIA for prepublication review and redaction all court papers or information they plan to

---

12. Exec. Order No. 12,333, § 1.8(h), 46 Fed. Reg. 59,941 (Dec. 4, 1981).

13. *Thompson*, case C. The attorneys to whom this footnote refers represented the wife of Thompson's deputy whom Thompson reported to the CIA for his admitted spouse abuse.

release to the public. The redaction process gives the Agency forewarning and prior control over all plaintiffs' court papers. Since no entity other than the CIA oversees the process, allowing the defendant-Agency this type of decision-making power over the complainant's materials opens the door for further abuse.

An Executive Order provides the guidelines for classifying documents and prohibits the classification of information simply because it is embarrassing to the government.[14] Nonetheless, the CIA often ignores this Order. A *Thompson* pleading footnote, for example, quoted a *Vanity Fair* magazine article that the plaintiff had reported misconduct by "now revealed spy Aldrich Ames." Embarrassed, the CIA deleted these quoted words, including the names of both Ames and the magazine, and insisted that the plaintiff merely allege that she had reported "a male contemporary."[15] This deletion occurred months after Ames' highly publicized arrest and a public acknowledgement by the CIA Director that Ames was a CIA employee.

Further, rather than complete its review and redaction of the *Thompson* complaint in a timely fashion, the Agency withheld the pleading for over 90 days. It forced the plaintiff's counsel to file the complaint under seal in order to comply with Title VII's statutory deadline for filing a civil action within 90 days after receipt of an Agency's Final Decision.[16]

The CIA also exploits secrecy agreements to intimidate lawyers. The CIA, for example in the *Doris* case, sent its security officers to warn opposing counsel that he had committed a security violation because he had referred in writing to an Agency document marked "administrative-internal use only."[17] The lawyer actually had done nothing wrong. Those not accustomed to working with classified information may not know that "administrative-internal use only" materials are not classified and using them is not a security violation. Unsuspecting lawyers, unaware that there are only three categories of classification—confidential, secret and top secret—thus are made to believe they have committed some type of security blunder.

Worse still, opposing counsel is led to believe that upon completion of the security clearance process, he/she will obtain from the CIA at least some of

---

14. Exec. Order No. 12,958, § 1.8(2), 60 Fed. Reg. 19,829 (Apr. 17, 1995). This order, issued by President Clinton, superseded the order issued by Ronald Reagan, which had a similar prohibition. Exec. Order No. 12,356, 47 Fed. Reg. 14,874 (Apr. 2, 1982).

15. *Thompson*, case C.

16. Title VII of the Civil Rights Act of 1964, 42 U.S.C. § 2000e-16, as amended Pub. L. No. 102-166, § 114(1) (1991).

17. *Doris*, case E.

the information needed to pursue a client's case. The CIA, however, almost always denies a complainant's attorney access to Agency information or records, even unclassified regulations and procedures, whether or not they have signed the Secrecy/Nondisclosure Agreement and received a CIA security clearance. Lawyers are duped into submitting control to the CIA of their client's legal action and receive nothing in return.

4. Misusing Security and Secrecy to Deny Access to Information, Evidence and Witnesses

a. Overly Broad Application of "Sources and Methods" Concept

The National Security Act of 1947 requires the CIA to protect "sources and methods."[18] Efforts by the CIA to avoid ordinary discovery and deny evidence to litigants often are based on the invocation of the need to safeguard sources and methods. The CIA legitimately must protect specific identities of sources, and there are certain methods, usually involving technological means of acquiring intelligence, that also should be protected. But the CIA would have the courts, Congress and the general public believe that "sources and methods" have a mystical, almost occult, quality that only the CIA is able to understand, define and protect.

In actuality, little is truly new or secret about many CIA sources and methods. Sources, the generic rather than the individual, and methods of intelligence collection are obvious. There is no mystery, or significant improvement from days gone by, about how to collect information on human beings. The media refers daily to spy satellites, electronic eavesdropping, code breaking, and the like. These "methods" of espionage are known worldwide. What must be protected are the details as to who or what exactly is the target, how that specific target is being attacked, and what equipment is being used.

Yet the CIA insists on guarding virtually all things in its domain, calling everything a "source" or "method," especially when Agency wrongdoing is threatened with exposure in the media or in a lawsuit. Thus the CIA can redact the name of Aldrich Ames from a pleading about to be filed in court after Ames had been arrested and publicly charged as a CIA employee engaged in selling secrets.[19] It does not matter that Ames was by then practically a house-

---

18. The National Security Act of 1947, § 103(c)(5), 50 U.S.C. § 403-3(c)(5) (West Supp. 2001).

19. *Thompson*, case C.

hold word, for the CIA seeks to protect equally the important and the unimportant, the publicly known and the still secret.

The CIA redacts the name of every city where it has a station or other covert office from all court documents although this information is common knowledge.[20] The Agency pretends that its does not have offices overseas, as though it could somehow carry out its mission to collect intelligence on foreign countries without having an overseas presence. Yet a number of retired male Chiefs of Station (COSs), who were associates of a consulting corporation in Washington, D.C., advertised in the corporation's brochure not only that they were former COSs, but also in which cities they were COSs. Contemporaneously, some of these same retired "old boys" were working at the CIA on contract as annuitants.

b. Denial of Access to Information and Evidence and State Secrets Privilege

Obtaining access to information necessary to support a legal case is a monumental task for a lawyer opposing a U.S. intelligence agency, particularly the CIA. The CIA controls virtually all the evidence. It is notorious for overclassification of information and perfunctorily classifies just about every piece of paper which it produces.[21] Even after a lawyer obtains a CIA security clearance and signs a secrecy agreement, the Agency still asserts secrecy and claims it has determined that opposing counsel has no "need to know" as the grounds to deny a complainant's attorney access to needed documentation and evidence. Moreover, the CIA groundlessly refuses to give cleared attorneys access to even unclassified information on CIA policies, procedures, and regulations. The determination whether or not to provide the requested material is purely a function of the arbitrary will of the CIA.

---

20. *Fitzgibbon v. CIA*, 911 F.2d 755 (D.C. Cir. 1990) (CIA could withhold station location previously disclosed in a congressional report).

21. There have been several law suits against the CIA for its broad and sweeping claims that its documents were classified and, therefore, exempt from disclosure under the Freedom of Information Act. For example, in *Fitzgibbon v. CIA*, 578 F. Supp. 704, 709 (D.D.C. 1983), the court compared the CIA's classification of documents to the FBI's. It pointed out that of 551 documents the CIA identified as related to those requested, the CIA turned over only 21 in their entirety. The FBI, on the other hand, winnowed down its claimed exemptions to parts of 13 documents and the full text of only one. Plaintiff contended throughout the litigation that the FBI was much more forthcoming with its records than the CIA, and this was borne out by available numbers. It was noted that the CIA does not contest this assessment, but offers reasons, such as the greater sensitivity attached to being a CIA source than an FBI source.

Worse still is the CIA's recent use of the state secrets privilege to deny access to information and evidence where the Director of the CIA, George Tenet, and/or his employees are the defendants. In two law suits, one of which was a garden variety gender discrimination case and the other a case alleging Fourth Amendment violations, Tenet invoked the little-known state secrets privilege and a formal claim of statutory privilege, pursuant to 50 U.S.C. §§403-3(c)(6) to thwart discovery and then prevail upon the courts to dismiss these cases.[22]

Historically, this privilege has been used with much circumspection to protect and safeguard only matters of real national security such as the most sensitive military secrets on missile technology and national reconnaissance. It has not been exploited to cover up constitutional violations and discrimination by a government agency or its personnel.

To invoke this privilege, the head of the agency which has control over the matter must merely assert that he personally considered it and that state secrets are involved which disclosure would jeopardize.[23] In one of the aforementioned cases, however, Tenet, not former Secretary of State, Madeleine Albright, asserted the privilege over a Department of State-written and controlled document, claiming it was a joint report because it was jointly investigated.[24] It was and rightly should have been only the prerogative of Secretary Albright to invoke this privilege.

Once the privilege is asserted, the CIA requests an in camera and ex parte review without the presence of opposing counsel or the plaintiffs even where they possess the same top secret security clearance as Tenet himself.[25] Tenet's exclusion of them is based on his decision, and his decision alone, that neither the plaintiffs nor their lawyers have the "need to know,"[26] albeit the plaintiffs' very right to sue pursuant to the Constitution is at stake. By claiming that the plaintiff and his or her lawyers have "no need to know," the CIA Director totally excludes the participation of any adversary.

At the same time, Tenet submits a declaration making sweeping claims that the national security of the U.S. would be seriously damaged if discovery were

---

22. *Tilden v. Tenet*, CA No. 00-987-A, 2000 U.S. Dist. LEXIS 20036 (E.D. Va. Dec. 6, 2000) (*Tilden I*), and *Horn v. Albright*, CA 94-1756 (D.D.C. 1994) (filed under seal in 1994), respectively, and 50 U.S.C. §403-3(c)(6) (West Supp. 2001); 50 U.S.C. §403(g) (West Supp. 2001).

23. *Tilden*, 2000 US Dist. LEXIS 20036, at *1.

24. *Horn v. Albright*, CA 94-1756 (D.D.C. 1994) (filed under seal in 1994).

25. *Tilden v. Tenet*, CA No. 00-987-A, 2000 U.S. Dist. LEXIS 20037, *5 (E.D. Va. Nov. 27, 2000) (*Tilden II*).

26. *Id.*

permitted.[27] In the gender discrimination case, he argued that "if disclosure is made, covert employees of the CIA will be compromised, CIA procedures will be disclosed, the ability to collect additional intelligence in certain areas will be jeopardized, foreign relations will be adversely impacted, and lives could be put in serious risk."[28]

Once the privilege is granted, the only remaining question is how or whether the case can proceed.[29] The CIA argues that the case must be dismissed if the plaintiff needs the information to pursue his or her case or if the CIA needs the information to defend itself. The CIA has successfully taken this tack in the conservative District Court for the Eastern District of Virginia.[30] A case filed in the District Court of the District of Columbia is still awaiting the judge's decision on the Agency's motion to dismiss.[31]

Although the Supreme Court has cautioned that the privilege "is not to be lightly invoked"[32] and generally the state secrets privilege is used to protect only the most sensitive national security and military secrets, the courts have refused to second-guess the CIA Director's assertion of the privilege.[33] The privilege, in effect, denies plaintiffs a forum under Article III of the Constitution for adjudication of their claims.[34] It allows a CIA Director's decision to take precedence over the U.S. Constitution. If abused, it is tantamount to granting the Agency and its employees absolute immunity from suit, even where their activities are illegal and/or discriminatory. This is a dangerous precedent indeed.

Many other examples exist of the CIA's attempts to prevent discovery and deny access to information and evidence. In the *Ellis* case, the CIA would not allow either Ellis or her cleared attorney access to any of Ellis' evidence that she had earmarked for possible litigation and that the CIA had required her to store in a CIA facility.[35] Ellis' attorney was informed that the CIA had determined it was unnecessary for him to review this information because the CIA deemed the material irrelevant. The lawyer, therefore, was forced to argue in district court against an Agency motion for dismissal without having even

---

27. *Id.* at *2.
28. *Id.* at *2–3.
29. *Id.* at *3.
30. *Id.*
31. *See supra* note 25.
32. *United States v. Reynolds*, 345 U.S. 1, 7 (1953).
33. *Tilden I*, 2000 US Dist. LEXIS 20036, at *3.
34. *Id.* at *3–4.
35. *Ellis*, case A.

looked at his client's evidence. The district court judge in the conservative Eastern District of Virginia did not even address this problem and agreed with the CIA to dismiss the case.

The denial of access to information and evidence apparently is becoming the CIA standard. In another recent case, the CIA refused to give opposing counsel the essential material which formed the basis for the client's suit.[36] The complainant's attorney was told that he did not need that information. Further, his request for Agency regulations governing the evidence which a cleared attorney was allowed to see was denied.

Another complainant was told that the CIA's OEEO investigator, a salaried employee of the defendant-CIA, would decide what material was appropriate for her and her counsel to use to support her case.[37] When determining the information the plaintiff and her lawyer would be allowed to see, the complainant was informed that the CIA's investigator would try to be responsive "unless he determines the information (which the plaintiff and the lawyer seek) is unnecessary."[38]

The lawyers in the *Thompson* case asked for the CIA regulations governing the Office of the Inspector General (OIG), which had investigated Thompson after she reported certain of her subordinates for wrongdoing, including alleged wife abuse.[39] Thompson also requested that information from her personnel file be released to her attorneys. Access to all of this information was denied, as was access to every other item of information which the lawyers requested and required to pursue the case. It was not until the CIA OEEO issued its Final Agency Decision, some two and one half years after Thompson filed her initial report of discrimination with the OEEO, that her attorneys were able to see a small part of the information they had requested. Counsel was never allowed to see their client's personnel file.

CIA security guidelines for discrimination claims state that employees do not have the right to Agency records even if they pertain to their own complaint.[40] They may not make copies from their official personnel files and may not use their position and access in search of material in support of their complaint.[41]

---

36. *M.K. I*, case F.
37. *Conway*, case G.
38. *Id.*
39. *Thompson*, case C. This case typifies the CIA's refusal to provide plaintiffs and counsel any of the requested information in discovery.
40. *See supra* note 6, at 3.
41. *Id.*

Further, the CIA's security guidelines state that the employee and his or her representative "may be authorized access" to the OEEO investigative report.[42] These guidelines fly in the face of EEOC's Management Directive for implementing Title VII. According to EEOC, the complainant and his or her counsel "must be" given access to the Agency's entire investigative report of the complaint.[43] The CIA's guidelines also may be in violation of both the complainant's constitutional guarantees to due process and federal rules and procedures since they obviously allow the CIA to deny the plaintiff and counsel their legal right to pertinent information and evidence.

Even after the long-awaited discovery process commences, the Agency invokes secrecy to deny access to evidence. On the basis of national security, almost all documentation requested in discovery is refused. Simple "yes" and "no" admissions are considered by the CIA to be secret and, likewise, are withheld. In the *Thompson* case, where the plaintiff had over twenty-five years of Clandestine Service experience with the CIA, the entire time working with classified information and herself classifying documents, she meticulously reviewed all admissions questions to ensure no question or answer would be classified.[44] Nevertheless, the Agency refused to respond to all but a few of the admissions on grounds of secrecy.

Unfortunately, the courts are loathe to force the CIA to disclose information in discovery, instead deferring to the Agency regarding what is and is not a matter of secrecy or national security.[45] CIA decisions, no matter how questionable, are allowed to stand, leaving the Agency, not the courts, the final arbiter as to whether information needed by the plaintiff in a law suit against the CIA can be withheld.[46] If the CIA says something is classified, it remains

---

42. *Id.* at 2.

43. EEO MD-110.

44. *Thompson*, case C.

45. *See, e.g., Halkin v. Helms,* 690 F.2d 977 (D.C. Cir. 1982); *CIA v. Sims,* 471 U.S. 159 (1985); *and supra* note 26 (FOIA cases). *See also* Phillip E. Hassman, Annotation, *What Matters are Exempt From Disclosure Under Freedom of Information Act (5 USCS § 552 (b)(1)) as "Specifically Authorized Under Criteria Established by an Executive Order to be Kept Secret in the Interest of National Defense or Foreign Policy",* 29 A.L.R. Fed. 606, 610 (1976), which points out that "Analysis of the cases discloses a reluctance on the part of judges to 'second-guess' Executive Branch officials when it comes to determining whether the release of information may be detrimental to the national security or foreign policy. Because of this, the 1974 amendment to the Freedom of Information Act is not likely to have a dramatic effect upon the disclosure of information...."

46. In *Weissman v. CIA,* 565 F.2d 692 (D.C. Cir. 1977), the Court of Appeals stated the "district court was correct in refusing to conduct an in camera inspection to check the ve-

classified and unavailable to the litigant. If, as a result, plaintiffs cannot pursue their lawsuit without the information or the CIA claims it needs the information to defend itself, the Agency argues that the case against it and its employees must be dismissed.

c. Denial of Access to Witnesses

In direct violation of federal discovery rules, the CIA denies opposing attorneys access to possible witnesses for the plaintiffs and refuses even to identify its witnesses.[47] Under the pretext of witness protection and requests for anonymity, reports produced by the CIA's Office of Security and the OIG generally do not identify witnesses or the specific evidence from these witnesses. Allegations made by unnamed and unknown witnesses are stated as facts. In this Kafkaesque environment, victims have no protection and no right to confront their accusers, let alone know who is saying what. In addition, the Agency even refuses to use an identity code to enable the sorting out of witnesses. A reader of an OIG report, therefore, does not know if one witness is making several accusations or if various witnesses are making the same allegation.

Secrecy allows the Agency to claim it has proof when, in fact, none exists. Thompson, for example, was falsely accused of sexually harassing an unnamed "male subordinate."[48] For two and a half years, under the guise of the need to protect its witnesses, the CIA continued this charade, refusing to reveal where and when such an incident occurred or provide the name of the alleged harassed male subordinate. Finally, during the discovery process, Department of Justice (DOJ) attorneys, charged with defending the CIA, revealed to Thompson's legal representatives that there was no male subordinate. Instead, a new story was concocted, and Thompson's lawyers were told that she had sexually harassed a male counterpart, the head of the DEA office in the country where Thompson was posted. When one of Thompson's attorneys contacted this man, he not only stated that the accusations against her were ab-

---

racity of CIA claims or to search for nonexempt material." *See also, Halperin v. CIA*, 446 F. Supp. 661 (D.D.C. 1978).

47. Fed. R. Civ. P. 26(a)(1) states "[a] party shall, without awaiting a discovery request, provide to other parties; (A) the name and, if known, the address and telephone number of each individual likely to have discoverable information relevant to disputed facts alleged with particularity in the pleading, identifying the subjects of information; (B) a copy of, or a description by category and location of, all documents, data compilations, and tangible things in the possession, custody, or control of the party that are relevent to the disputed facts alleged with particularity in the pleadings...."

48. *Thompson*, case C.

solutely untrue, but also provided an affidavit averring that Thompson never in any way or at any time sexually harassed him and always conducted herself in a thoroughly professional manner. He noted also that no one from the CIA had ever interviewed or even talked to him about Thompson. The very same day that Thompson's lawyers presented this affidavit to the CIA's attorneys, the government settled the case in Thompson's favor.

5. Attempting to Exert Control over Employee's Attorney-Client Information

Under the guise of the need for secrecy, the CIA insists on control and storage in a CIA building of information related to a suit or potential suit. In an employment discrimination case, for example, the Agency assigns the complainant and his or her lawyer a safe at a CIA facility, reviews and screens all material prior to transporting it to the facility, decides what documents the attorney will be allowed to see, transports these documents to the assigned safe, escorts the attorney while he or she reads the information, and then reviews and confiscates, if deemed necessary, any notes taken by the attorney before counsel can depart the facility.[49]

This process raises serious concerns about the CIA's access to and control of privileged attorney-client information, opposing counsel's notes and drafts, internal memoranda, and work product. Also, forcing lawyers to travel to an Agency facility in Virginia to perform their jobs is time-consuming, costly and inconvenient. The law firm for the CIA women's class action case agreed to such a cumbersome process and found themselves confined to a small room at CIA headquarters, given an Agency safe to which the CIA had the combination for storage of their material and accompanied by Agency-hired guards even to the cafeteria and the bathroom.[50]

In the *Thompson* case, the Agency insisted that her lawyers use computers within the OEEO at CIA headquarters to prepare their case documentation.[51] The CIA also demanded Thompson's case-related information be stored in the OEEO. Her attorneys refused since the information which formed the basis of the Thompson case was unclassified and Thompson's counsel already were passwording, compartmentalizing and limiting access to the case. To store Thompson's information, in fact, her lawyers had rented the same type of safe

---

49. *See supra* note 6, at 2 and 3.
50. *Class Action*, case D.
51. *Thompson*, case C.

used by the courts and the CIA, a safe made specifically for the retention of classified documentation.

Compliance with this CIA-controlled process may result in another very serious problem for employees and counsel. The CIA capriciously may decide and has decided not to allow complainants and their representatives access to their material stored at the Agency facility.[52] In *Doris*, the CIA placed a new twist on the matter of controlling a complainant's information. It arbitrarily arrived at the determination that Doris was not allowed to see the case-related material which she had been required to keep in an Agency facility, but that her lawyer could review it without her.[53] Given the CIA's unique and purposely obscure way of preparing documentation, a lawyer may not be able to interpret what he is looking at or its significance without the client's presence.

6. Maintaining Special Relationship with Judges in Virginia

According to a former attorney in the CIA's OGC, whom the author interviewed in 1999, Agency lawyers have regular, ongoing contact with judges, particularly in the state of Virginia.[54] "The federal judges in the Eastern District of Virginia are like one of us (CIA lawyers)," he stated. "We call and consult them and they call us."[55] In view of this collegial environment, plaintiffs suing the CIA are indeed disadvantaged when the venue is Virginia.[56]

The judges in Virginia, where CIA headquarters and most of its other facilities are located, reputedly are conservative. Their consistently pro-CIA decisions lend credibility to the concept that a special relationship exists between Virginia judges and the CIA.

In the CIA's class action fairness hearing the federal judge in the Eastern District of Virginia District Court decided to force acceptance of a pro-Agency, allegedly negotiated, settlement upon the women, although all but one class agent opposed this settlement.[57] In the *Ellis* case, another judge in the Eastern District of Virginia admitted to the court that she had made up her mind to dismiss the

---

52. *See supra* Chapter One, A.4.b. for a discussion on denial of access to information and evidence stored at a CIA facility to the plaintiff and her attorney in Ellis, case A.

53. *Doris*, case E.

54. This former OGC attorney asked for anonymity.

55. *Id.* (the same former OGC attorney is quoted here).

56. The CIA has succeeded in having Title VII cases transferred to the District Court for the Eastern District of Virginia.

57. *Class Action*, case D.

case as the CIA had requested before Ellis' attorney spoke.[58] The judge even denied the attorney's request to amend the Ellis complaint, although it had never before been amended and the CIA had not filed a responsive pleading.

Proving a special relationship and ex parte discussions between Virginia judges and the CIA is difficult, however. Ex parte, by its very nature, is one-sided, "for the benefit of one party only and without notice to…any person adversely interested."[59]

Nonetheless, on at least one occasion which can be cited here, the CIA intervened in a legal proceeding and had an ex parte contact with a Virginia judge. This case involved a CIA employee who had allegedly beaten his foreign-born wife and was embroiled in a divorce suit.[60] In an effort to assist its employee and avoid or delay the embarrassment of this case, a CIA OGC attorney intervened and asked the judge's permission to return the Agency husband to his overseas post before the divorce suit was settled. Although the wife had no representation during this conversation, the judge agreed to the CIA's request and the wife was forced to wait to obtain a divorce until her estranged spouse returned to the United States a year later. Concerning this same employee, the CIA also reportedly intervened to have the wife's report of child and spouse abuse removed from Alexandria, Virginia police records and destroyed on grounds of "national security."[61] Adding salt to the wound, the court placed a gag order on the wife, her friends, her agents and anyone speaking on her behalf, prohibiting any discussion of the child or wife abuse.

As explained in above Section A.4.b on the Denial of Access to Information and Evidence, the CIA also uses in camera and ex parte review and excludes opposing counsel and plaintiffs when it asserts the state's secret privilege. This type of action opens the door for misconduct and abuse.

7. Using Obstructive and Delaying Tactics

The CIA's OGC is composed of scores of Agency lawyers who receive their government salaries no matter how long it takes to resolve a case. If one lawyer

---

58. *Ellis*, case A.

59. *Black's Law Dictionary Abridged*, 399 (6th ed. 1994).

60. *Thompson*, case C.

61. In *Doris*, case E, the CIA similarly intervened and insisted that Doris's Congressman destroy her correspondence to him, although Doris was an overt CIA employee and her letter to her Congressman consisted only of unclassified information about adverse actions the CIA had taken against her. The Congressman complied with the CIA's instructions.

leaves, he is merely replaced by another. There is nothing in the system that promotes the expeditious resolution of cases and complaints when the Agency is the defendant or the potential defendant.

On the contrary, a practice of obstructing and delaying legal action has worked to the CIA's advantage for many years. Potential employee-litigants living on government wages, especially lower-salaried women and minorities, generally do not have the financial or emotional wherewithal to carry out protracted suits against the CIA. The repeated, unnecessary delays and obstructions are expensive and demoralizing. After a while, many employees subjected to this treatment are cowed or simply give up.

The CIA rarely meets a deadline; instead, it may request additional time from the plaintiff or totally ignore regulations. This practice contrasts with the strict timeliness standards to which complainants are held. Employees in discrimination cases, for example, must meticulously abide by each and every time limit established by Title VII and the CIA. There is no forgiveness or equitable modification for the victim's lateness—one day late and the complaint is thrown out.

The CIA OEEO's Final Decisions are routinely late, frequently because the CIA fails to complete (or start) its investigations in a timely manner. Consequently, beleaguered complainants find themselves being either placed in the position of granting the CIA lengthy extensions or called uncooperative.

In *Conway*, after the expiration of the 180 days allowed by federal regulations for the CIA to produce its final investigative report, the CIA's OEEO requested another 90 days.[62] She agreed, contingent on the OEEO also investigating her harassment complaints, which the CIA had taken out of the OEEO process without her consent and investigated under an unclassified Agency internal regulation, AR 9-2.[63] The CIA did not respond concerning the contingency, but took the additional time and much more.

The CIA's delays have resulted in more than doubling time limitations established under federal law. For example, although the total time allowed to complete the internal administrative procedures pursuant to Title VII amounts to about one year, the CIA's delays and obstructions prevented *Thompson* from filing in federal court for well over two years.[64]

Further, under the attorney's secrecy agreement with the CIA, counsel must submit all potential court documents to the Agency for redaction before fil-

---

62. *Conway*, case G.

63. Conway objected to this CIA maneuver to investigate her case under AR 9-2, thereby, denying her due process and circumventing the protections guaranteed under Title VII. Her objection fell on deaf ears.

64. *Thompson*, case C.

ing this material in court. In *Thompson*, the CIA provided numerous, contradictory excuses for delaying the redaction process.[65] As time passed, Thompson and her attorneys worried that the Agency purposely would not return the pleading in time to meet the 90-day deadline, pursuant to Title VII. Then on the 89th day in a transparent attempt to produce further delay, the CIA changed one unimportant word of its Final Decision and sent the "amended" Decision to Thompson's attorneys, stating the Agency was "granting" another 90 days due to the amendment.

In *Thompson* also, the CIA filed a motion in the district court asking for a dismissal of all but the Title VII counts. The judge refused, stating in a court order, "it appears…that actions which could be construed in furtherance of the conspiracy which caused harm to the plaintiff occurred within one year prior to filing the complaint."[66] The CIA's lawyers, surprised at losing, then filed another motion requesting the same judge to reconsider. The Agency's lawyers warned the plaintiff's attorneys that they would appeal the decision to the Fourth Circuit Court of Appeals, the Fourth Circuit Court of Appeals sitting en banc, and the Supreme Court, if necessary. They had nothing to lose if the process took years. Thompson, on the other hand, would be forced to continue her already lengthy and costly struggle against the CIA.

Even after a case against the CIA is settled in favor of the complainant and agreements are signed, employees and their attorneys face more obstruction. Employee awards are delayed and attorneys may have to litigate in court to obtain their promised reasonable attorney fees. The preparatory paper work necessary for the government to issue the funds to pay compensatory damages in the *Thompson* case was not even started until Thompson's attorneys began applying pressure through the DOJ.[67] Then the Agency claimed to lack the institutional knowledge regarding how to deposit the check in Thompson's true name bank account, because Thompson had retired under cover. Imagine the CIA claiming not to know how to clandestinely deposit funds! It took four months, much prodding and media publicity before the CIA finally paid Thompson. Her lawyers had to battle the Agency in court for their fees and were finally paid nine months after the settlement.[68]

In *Ellis*, the EEOC judge held that the Agency must post a clear and visible statement on all bulletins boards in CIA buildings where announcements are

---

65. *Id.*
66. *Id.*
67. *Id.*
68. *Thompson v. Woolsey*, CA No. 94-923-A (E.D. Va. Apr. 25, 1995) (unpublished opinion).

normally posted to the effect that the CIA was in violation of Title VII and had been ordered by the court to discontinue discriminatory practices against women.[69] The judge also ordered the CIA to pay reasonable attorney fees to Ellis' attorney. CIA lawyers took the next two years appealing to EEOC to reconsider its decision. The CIA lost and then allowed at least two months to pass before it posted in one small corner of an obscure bulletin board the required statement. One CIA employee commented that she would never have noticed the statement had she not been looking for it every day. In violation of the court order, the statement did not appear on all Agency bulletin boards where notices are normally posted. The CIA then refused to pay Ellis' attorney fees and again requested the EEOC to reconsider its decision regarding fees. These lengthy appeals processes punished the plaintiff and her lawyer, not the bureaucrats working in the CIA's OGC.

In the case involving the woman who was told she was too attractive and strong-willed to be sent to a certain overseas post, the CIA agreed to settle immediately after its manager was caught in a blatant lie.[70] The manager had denied making any comment about the female employee's attractiveness and strong will, but a CIA OEEO counselor admitted under oath that the manager had told her that he indeed had made that statement. Nevertheless, the Agency delayed and argued with the woman and her attorney for nearly a year before finalizing and signing the settlement agreement.

B. Other Impediments to Attempts to Redress Grievances

Employees in the CIA who file formal complaints generally are those who are powerless and see no other way out. They seek relief through avenues ostensibly established by the Agency to help aggrieved parties, and they place their hopes for resolution and justice in the hands of grievance officers or OEEO counselors. Unfortunately for the complainant, OIG and OEEO officers are not neutral, independent or impartial. They are employed and paid by the CIA. Complainants find that the doors of redress are closed or were never really opened. These employees are damaged even further because they dared to speak out. The CIA uses tactics such as retaliation, reprisals, and isolation to punish and stop them. Those with the responsibility and power to

---

69. *Ellis*, case A.
70. *Hannah*, case H.

assist, especially CIA managers within the OIG, Office of Medical Services (OMS), OEEO, OGC, and the Office of Security, may collude and conspire against them. Cover, secrecy and the Agency's exemption from the Whistle-blower Protection Act (on grounds of national security[71]) prevent employees from letting the outside world know what is really happening.

1. Collusion, Complicity and Reprisals

a. Complicity of Inspector General's Office

Examples of collusion, retaliation, and reprisals within the OIG are many. The OIG often has gone after the victim, rather than the offender. The following recaps but a few cases in which apparent OIG misconduct has occurred:

Jill, case J—Jill's case is perhaps the most egregious. The victim of an attempted rape and beating at the hands of another CIA officer, Jill became the target of an OIG investigation when she and her Agency husband filed an OEEO complaint and insisted that the would-be rapist be reported to the DOJ for possible criminal prosecution. The OIG tried to whitewash the matter. Although the assailant admitted the attempted rape and battery, the OIG report blamed the female victim, indicating she was emotionally unstable and had invited the attempted rape.

Hannah, case H—Hannah was investigated by the OIG in retaliation for filing a gender discrimination complaint. The OIG falsely accused her of visa fraud but was forced to drop the charges when Hannah won her case.

Doris, case E—Doris filed grievances with both the CIA's OEEO and the OIG. The OIG turned these complaints against her, making her the target of an investigation. The OIG then refused to show her or her lawyer its final report once Doris pointed out errors in an earlier OIG report. The OIG also confiscated the notes that Doris had taken on the earlier report. After Doris was placed on administrative leave, she was advised by the OIG to resign and threatened that if she did not and were fired, she would find it very difficult to find future work anywhere else.

Thompson, case C—Thompson had her headquarters senior assignment and promised COS posting withdrawn and every avenue of redress closed in her face by the OIG in retaliation for reporting her deputy for alleged wife abuse. She then was accused by the OIG of sexually harassing some unnamed male subordinate. When Thompson offered to take a polygraph on the issue,

---

71. WPA, Pub. L. No. 101-12, §3(i), 103 Stat. 16 (Apr. 10, 1989); 5 U.S.C. §1201 (1996).

the OIG refused the request. Thompson was told by the OIG investigator that she probably had no way of proving herself innocent. The OIG also refused to pay heed to numerous affidavits from other CIA officers, the United States Ambassador and Department of State diplomats who served abroad with Thompson, attesting to her professionalism and character, as well as the non-occurrence of any incident or type of harassment.

Ira, case I—Ira, a former COS in Europe, tried to report the Inspector General (IG) for wrongdoing to the Director of the Central Intelligence Agency (DCI). As a result, Ira's promised future assignment disappeared and his career was in effect terminated.

The OIG not only has retaliated against employees who are victims of possible crimes by Agency officers, but it also has not reported the information to the DOJ, as required. In an OIG report on the Agency handling of a problem concerning the battered wife of a CIA employee at an overseas station, the OIG took the position that such matters were mere domestic quarrels to be worked out by husband and wife.[72] The OIG decided that assault of a spouse on United States government property overseas, even federally-leased housing, was not under federal jurisdiction and, therefore, need not be reported to the DOJ for possible prosecution. It took the courageous and unswerving efforts of a female Agency officer to provide the internal memoranda, documentary information, and the legal precedents necessary to show federal housing overseas may indeed be considered federal jurisdiction.[73] In return for her efforts, the OIG recommended that OGC take action against this employee.[74]

b. Complicity of Office of Medical Services

The OMS is another Agency entity that appears to punish those who dare to complain. This Office, in fact, spearheaded the case against *Ellis*.[75] Indirect psychological assessments have been conducted by OMS on employees who speak out and report wrongdoing. OMS has placed psychiatric medical holds on complainants without their knowledge, precluding them from obtaining overseas assignments. Since a successful career in the CIA's Clandestine Service generally depends on foreign work, a medical hold may well prevent an

---

72. CIA Inspector Gen. Rep. 92-134-IG (1992).

73. This Agency officer demonstrated that pursuant to 18 U.S.C. §7(7) (West Supp. 2000) defining special maritime and territorial jurisdiction, federal jurisdiction may have applied because the alleged offender was a United States national.

74. Annex to CIA Inspector Gen. Rep., 92-134-IG (1993).

75. *Ellis*, case A.

employee's professional progress and promotions. It may even effectively terminate an individual's career.

The OMS performed indirect psychological assessments on at least three Clandestine Service employees mentioned in this book after they filed complaints with the CIA's OEEO:

Betty, case B—Betty reported her Agency spouse for beating her and was told that she was being disruptive. An OMS psychologist was sent overseas to interview her on the pretext of discussing her husband's violent behavior. As a result of the interview, the Agency placed a medical hold on her. It was not until she tried to obtain another overseas assignment that she learned of the medical hold.

Hannah, case H—Similarly, in the case of the "attractive" *Hannah*, OMS placed a medical hold on her after she filed an OEEO complaint. At the same time the OIG initiated an investigation of her and accused her of visa fraud.

Doris, case E—This collusion between the OIG and OMS was apparent also in *Doris*. She filed an OEEO complaint, became the target of an OIG investigation and had a medical hold placed on her subsequent to an OMS psychiatrist conducting an indirect psychological assessment of her without her knowledge or participation. As with Betty, Doris was characterized as disruptive.

The OMS, OIG, and certain CIA managers seem to take lightly reports of domestic violence. The abused, rather than the abuser, has been required to undergo psychiatric evaluation. *Katherine*, for example, who was not a CIA employee, was returned to a CIA facility and made to undergo an OMS examination after she reported her CIA husband for beating her.[76] Although she had shown her wounds and bruises to the COS and appealed to him for help, the COS and OMS thought something was wrong with her rather than her batterer-husband.

c. Office of Equal Employment Opportunity, As Part of Problem

The CIA's OEEO appears to be part of the problem rather than the solution. Its full-time staff members generally are CIA employees on rotational assignments from other Agency components to which they must return after completing their stints in the OEEO. They are neither independent nor neutral.

An OEEO counselor admitted to the author that over 98 percent of the OEEO's Final Decisions favor the CIA, rather than the complainant.[77] This means that those in so-called protected categories who file employment discrimination

---

76. *Katherine*, case K.

77. The OEEO counselor requested anonymity. The CIA's OEEO is supposed to file these statistics with EEOC annually.

complaints with the CIA's OEEO have almost no chance of internally resolving problems in their favor. They place their hopes in the fairness and integrity of the OEEO when, in reality, there is little or no hope of impartiality.

Moreover, the OEEO investigations invariably take more than twice the amount of time that EEOC's Management Directive allows.[78] Often the employee's allegations are dismissed without good reason. An appeal of the OEEO's dismissal must wait until the Final Agency Decision is received and the plaintiff is finally allowed to proceed to EEOC or district court.

The *Conway* case is a good example of what a complainant may face if he or she brings an employment discrimination grievance to the CIA's OEEO.[79] When Conway initially made contact with the OEEO, she was advised by the OEEO counselor and the Chief of Complaints that she did not need a lawyer and retaining an attorney would be a waste of her money. Nevertheless, pursuant to federal regulations and procedures, she chose to exercise her right to be represented at every stage of the complaint process.[80] She requested that OEEO postpone the pre-complaint counseling stage until her lawyer(s) could obtain a CIA security clearance and that the Agency grant clearances to two representatives rather than one. The OEEO denied both requests, forcing Conway to prepare her own issues and bases without the assistance of counsel but with the "assistance" of an OEEO counselor. Then the OEEO unilaterally reworded her allegations and summarily dismissed them.

In *Conway* and other cases, the OEEO purposely has circumvented the protections granted and guaranteed to aggrieved parties under Title VII[81] and, without the agreement of complainants, transferred cases to so-called harassment investigators who review complaints pursuant to an internal CIA regulation, AR 9-2. As a result, complainants are further disadvantaged and denied their right to an expeditious OEEO investigation and an investigative report.

Conway, to no avail, protested the transfer of two of her complaints to a harassment investigator under AR 9-2. The untrained harassment investigator refused to allow Conway to be represented by counsel on the grounds that she was limiting the meetings and proceedings to those with a "need to know."

Additionally, in violation of federal procedures and regulations,[82] the investigator did not advise Conway of her rights and responsibilities at the ini-

---

78. EEO MD-110.
79. *Conway*, case G.
80. EEO MD-110.
81. Title VII of the Civil Rights Act of 1964, 42 U.S.C. §2000e-16, *as amended* Pub. L. No. 102-166, §114(1) (1991).
82. 29 C.F.R. §1614 (2000) and EEO MD-110.

tial counseling session or at any time thereafter or that she was to receive in writing within 30 calendar days of the first counseling contact the notice of her right to file a formal complaint within 15 days of the receipt of that notice. The investigator refused to conduct a final interview with Conway within 30 days of the initial contact and, in fact, refused to grant and never granted her final interview. Without requesting an extension, the investigator delayed to the point that she was severely delinquent in completing both inquiries—she did not complete the inquiry into Conway's first complaint until over two months after it was due and the second investigation was finished five months late.

Moreover, when Conway tried to have her complaints transferred back to the OEEO after the AR 9-2 processing was unsatisfactorily completed, the OEEO, again in violation of federal rules and procedures, refused to allow her to file a formal complaint based on her original allegations.[83] After a substantial delay in time, the OEEO unilaterally and without the agreement of the complainant reworded both of Conway's complaints and incorrectly redefined the issues to state that she alleged management did not conduct a thorough and impartial investigation of her harassment complaints. The OEEO reframed the claims to reflect what it wanted them to say, rather than what Conway alleged.

The CIA's OEEO appears to work hand and glove with the OIG and the OGC to the disadvantage of victims. Often, as noted above under Chapter One, Section B.1.a, entitled "Complicity of the Inspector General's Office," once an employee files an OEEO claim, the OIG makes him or her the target of an investigation. The OGC also becomes involved as an adversary to complainants at most stages of the OEEO process, including but not limited to, the clearances for lawyers, the redaction of information, the refusal to give the complainant's counsel access to information and witnesses and the settlement negotiations, if any. The CIA's OEEO is not a neutral, impartial body but part of this system that continues and perpetuates discrimination.

2. False Allegations

Employees, especially women, of the CIA who report wrongdoing or file grievances may find themselves subjected to false accusations of sexual promis-

---

83. Pursuant to 29 C.F.R. § 1614 (2000) and EEO MD-110, the aggrieved person, not the EEO counselor, must decide whether to file formal complaint and the counselor must make certain the aggrieved person understands that she may file a formal complaint.

cuity, homosexuality and alcoholism.[84] Since the United States government is immune from suits for slander and libel unless it waives immunity, there is little that an individual can accomplish through the legal process to restore his or her reputation.[85] Moreover, although such allegations ruin careers, factually they are difficult, if not impossible, to disprove and denial is ineffective.

For CIA women accusations of being sexually active are the grist for hurtful rumors, gossip and negative "hall files." The same is not true for men.[86] The myth is that men are able to handle sexual relationships and remain in control, but women lose control. Worse than accusations of sexual promiscuity, however, are allegations of homosexuality, since even admitted homosexuality has precluded employment by the CIA until recently.

Moreover, if a woman drinks alcoholic beverages, she may be confronted with accusations of alcoholism. Yet Aldrich Ames was found lying drunk in the streets of Rome by the Italian police and no action was taken against him by the CIA. The Agency will not accept alcohol evaluations from "outside" (non-CIA affiliated) doctors and experts. Instead, to clear oneself, an employee must undergo a CIA OMS evaluation which, in view of the collusion among various CIA offices, is likely to be influenced by other Agency entities that have a stake in "proving" themselves right.

3. Methods to Prevent Aggrieved Parties from Speaking Out

CIA employees are well aware that reporting wrongdoing internally can result in career suicide, retaliation, cover up and inaction regarding the reported problem. Some individuals have wanted to speak out publicly in hopes of righting these abuses. Systematic and continuous warnings, however, are issued in writing by CIA management prohibiting Agency employees from talking to the media. A CIA employee must fill out an "outside activity report" on any media contact. Only the CIA's Public Affairs Office is permitted access to the press.

---

84. *Thompson*, case C; *Lilah*, case L; and *Mary Ann*, case M.

85. Under the Federal Tort Claims Act of 1946, 28 U.S.C.A. sections 2674 and 2680(h) (West 1994), the United States is not liable for any claim arising out of libel or slander.

86. Interestingly, the CIA's male macho population is notorious for sexual misconduct. The CIA's *Glass Ceiling Study* reported that while 50 percent of the Agency women admitted to being sexually harassed by male supervisors, less than two percent reported the harassment for fear of retaliation. Prof'l Res. Inc. & Hubbard & Revo-Cohen, Inc., CIA, Glass Ceiling Study (1992).

Those who work under official cover are ostensibly employed by other government agencies or commercial entities. Cover supposedly enables them to operate more clandestinely and with less public exposure than if they identified themselves as CIA. Cover, however, too often is used to mask wrongdoing and prevent Agency officers from speaking out, lest they violate their cover.

Some of the women in the class action against the Agency dared to appear on television to publicly discuss the CIA's sex discrimination.[87] The television network shadowed their faces and muffled their voices to conceal their identities. They hid to protect themselves from the CIA, not from foreign enemies.

Most Agency employees who work under cover during their CIA careers are allowed to drop cover and retire as overt Agency officers. Those who have reported wrongdoing, however, have been forced to retain their cover and retire as employees of another United States Government agency, rather than the CIA, to prevent them from going public with reports of CIA wrongdoing. A person under cover cannot tell what he or she knows about CIA wrongdoing because the individual supposedly never worked for the CIA.

When *Thompson* chose to retire, the CIA forced her to leave under the cover of another government agency to prevent her from discussing Agency misconduct.[88] This maneuver was a clear abuse of cover. Thompson had been identified in her true name as a CIA officer in at least 200 articles in the United States press and in dozens of articles in newspapers abroad, as well as on several television programs and National Public Radio. In addition, during her career the CIA itself had declared her as a CIA officer to ten different foreign governments with whom she worked in liaison. She also was known as a CIA officer to the Russians, the East Europeans, the Cubans and the Chinese, and in the 1970s and 1980s was identified in true name as CIA in at least two left-leaning foreign publications. Thompson in reality had no cover. What was foisted upon her was a CIA effort to cover up.

* * *

U.S. Intelligence Agencies send their message loud and clear:
Lawyers and clients beware. These Agencies, and particularly the CIA, will do everything in their power to make you sorry you ever sought justice.

---

87. *Class action*, case D.

88. *Thompson*, case C. In its rush to settle the *Thompson* case, the government forgot to include a gag order as one of the settlement terms. Hence the CIA tried to maintain the fiction that Thompson worked for another government agency to keep Thompson quiet about CIA wrongdoing.

Chapter Two

Sovereign Immunity

Intelligence agencies and their officers almost always try to have a case against them dismissed on grounds of immunity. At the very least, they argue for qualified immunity, claiming that they reasonably believed the actions in question were lawful. Consequently, plaintiffs and their lawyers need to be prepared to show that the laws which the defendants violated were clearly established.

A. Background

Historically, this country has espoused the principle that neither private citizen nor government official, no matter how lofty or pedestrian, may stand above the Constitution and laws of the United States. Our heritage is rooted in the best of English law and theory, as exemplified in Blackstone's Commentaries, "[I]t is a general and indisputable rule, that where there is a legal right, there is also a legal remedy by suit, or action at law, whenever that right is invaded... [E]very right, when withheld, must have a remedy, and every injury its proper redress."[1]

In *Marbury v. Madison*, Chief Justice Marshall affirmed that our young democratic nation would follow this tradition when he delivered the Supreme Court's opinion:

> The very essence of civil liberty consists in the right of every individual to claim protection of the laws, whenever he receives an injury.... The government of the United States has been emphatically termed a government of laws, and not of men. It will certainly cease to deserve this appellation, if the laws furnish no remedy for violation of a vested legal right.[2]

---

1. 3 William Blackstone, Commentaries *23, *109.
2. *Marbury v. Madison*, 5 U.S. (1 Cranch) 137, 163 (1803).

Almost eighty years later, in *United States v. Lee*, the Supreme Court specifically applied this principle to federal officials, precedentially denting the government's claim to sovereign immunity. The Court held:

> no man in this country is so high that he is above the law.... All the officers of the government from the highest to the lowest, are creatures of the law and are bound to obey it.[3]

B. Contemporary Application of Immunity

Despite the occasional lofty pronouncements of the Supreme Court, the government's unrestricted right to immunity continued until 1946, when absolute immunity was legislatively terminated with the passage of the Federal Tort Claims Act.[4] Even with the passage of this Act, however, Congress carefully circumscribed the type of torts for which the United States government would be liable, specifically excepting claims arising out of libel, slander, misrepresentation and deceit.[5]

Then in 1971, the Supreme Court took a momentous step toward holding federal government officers responsible for their illegal conduct. In *Bivens v. Six Unknown Federal Narcotics Agents*, it found that when federal agents, acting under color of law, violate a person's Fourth Amendment rights, the victim, upon proof of injury, is entitled to recover money damages.[6] Later, the Supreme Court extended its decision regarding Fourth Amendment violations to cover other unconstitutional acts for which federal officials may be held personally liable.[7]

Bivens, however, purposely left unanswered the question of whether federal officials were immune from liability by virtue of their official position. Six years later in *Butz v. Economou*, this important issue was addressed.[8] *Butz v. Economou* observed that the cause of action recognized in *Bivens* would be

---

3. *United States v. Lee*, 106 U.S. 196, 261 (1882).

4. The Federal Tort Claims Act of 1946, 28 U.S.C.A. §§ 2671, 2674, 2680 (West 1994).

5. *Id.* at sections 2674 and 2680(h) states, "The United States shall be liable, respecting the provisions of this title relating to tort claims...Exceptions...(h) any claim arising out of...libel, slander, misrepresentation, deceit...."

6. *Bivens v. Six Unknown Fed. Narcotics Agents*, 403 U.S. 388, 390 (1971).

7. *See* Chapter Six on *Bivens*.

8. *Butz v. Economou*, 438 U.S. 478 (1978).

meaningless should federal officials be entitled to absolute immunity for their constitutional transgressions.[9] The Court reasoned that:

> If…all officials exercising discretion were exempt from personal liability, a suit under the Constitution could provide no redress to the injured citizen, nor would it in any degree deter federal officials from committing constitutional wrongs. Moreover, no compensation would be available from the Government, for the (Federal) Tort Claims Act prohibits recovery for injuries stemming from discretionary acts, even when that discretion has been abused.[10]

Having determined that a plaintiff is entitled to a remedy in damages for unconstitutional actions against him or her, the Court understood that it then had to examine how to reconcile the plaintiff's right to compensation with the need to protect the decision-making process of government agencies.[11]

The Supreme Court Justices in *Butz v. Economou*, therefore, took a hard look at the question of immunity and whether, as the United States argued, federal government officials should be entitled to absolute immunity even if they infringe upon a plaintiff's constitutional rights and the violation was knowing and deliberate.[12] The Court determined that in a suit for damages arising out of constitutional violations federal officials exercising discretion are entitled only to qualified immunity, subject to those "exceptional situations" where absolute immunity is essential for the conduct of public business.[13] Although the Court noted that government officials would not be liable for mere mistakes in judgment, it held they generally may not discharge their duties in a manner they know or should know violates the Constitution or transgresses clearly established constitutional rules.[14]

The Court also noted that our system rests on the assumption that all people, whatever their position in government, are subject to federal laws.[15] In view of this principle, it concluded that federal officials seeking absolute immunity from liability for their unconstitutional actions must bear the burden of establishing that public policy requires that exemption.[16]

---

9. *Id.* at 501.
10. *Id.* at 505.
11. *Id.* at 503
12. *Id.* at 485.
13. *Id.* at 507.
14. *Id.*
15. *Id.* at 506.
16. *Id.*

The Court recognized a limited group of executive officials who needed absolute immunity. This category included judges and prosecutors, as well as those performing adjudicatory functions within federal agencies and agency attorneys in conducting trials and presenting evidence.[17]

In 1982, the Supreme Court further defined the scope of the government's absolute, as well as qualified or "good faith," immunity in *Harlow v. Fitzgerald.*[18] The Court identified officials whose special functions or constitutional status required complete protection from suit. It held that those entitled to absolute immunity were: legislators in their legislative functions, judges in their judicial functions; and certain Executive Branch officials including the President of the United States, prosecutors and individuals engaged in adjudicative functions.[19] The Court, however, pointed out that for all other executive officials, qualified, not absolute, immunity represented the norm.[20]

Also in *Harlow*, the Court purged qualified immunity of its subjective element and focused the substantive standard for qualified immunity on an objective test. It applied the test of the objective legal reasonableness of a federal official's conduct, as measured by clearly established law. The Court stated, "If the law is clearly established, the immunity defense ordinarily should fail, since a reasonably competent public official should know the law governing his conduct."[21] Basically, if a federal official knew or should have known that his conduct violated clearly established statutory or constitutional rights, the official would be liable for civil damages. Justice Brennan, in his concurring opinion, explained, "We...hold that government officials performing discretionary functions generally are shielded from liability for civil damages insofar as their conduct does not violate clearly established statutory or constitutional rights of which a reasonable person would have known."[22]

The very limited circumstances under which a federal official would be entitled to absolute immunity were evidenced in *Mitchell v. Forsyth* by the Supreme Court's ruling that the Attorney General's national security functions did not warrant absolute immunity.[23] While serving as Attorney General, John Mitchell authorized a warrantless wiretap for the purposes of gathering intelligence on the activities of an alleged radical group which threatened the se-

---

17. *Id.* at 508–517.
18. *Harlow v. Fitzgerald*, 457 U.S. 800, 806-17 (1982).
19. *Id.* at 806–07.
20. *Id.* at 807.
21. *Id.* at 818–19.
22. *Id.* at 821.
23. *Mitchell v. Forsyth*, 472 U.S. 511 (1985).

curity of the United States. Upon learning of the wiretap, Forsyth filed a civil action against Mitchell and others, claiming that the technical surveillance to which he was subjected violated his Fourth Amendment rights which prohibited warrantless wiretaps in cases involving threats to national security.[24]

On appeal, the Supreme Court addressed the question of whether the Attorney General's actions, taken in furtherance of national security, were shielded from scrutiny in civil damage suits by absolute immunity similar to that invested in the President, judges, prosecutors, and officials performing quasi-judicial functions.[25] The Court, in its decision, first noted that the status of a Cabinet official was not in itself sufficient to afford the Attorney General absolute immunity.[26] The claim to absolute immunity must rest not on a position within the Executive Branch but on the nature of the function being performed.[27] The Court pointed out that Mitchell, in authorizing the wiretap, was not acting in his prosecutorial capacity and that the functional approach to absolute immunity provided scant support for "blanket immunization" of the Attorney General's performance in carrying out tasks essential to the national security function.[28]

Second, the Court recognized that national security functions were carried out in secret and, therefore, generally did not subject federal officials to the risks of vexatious litigation as did judicial and prosecutorial duties.[29] On the contrary, the Court acknowledged, it was far more likely that in carrying out national security tasks, actual abuses would not give rise to litigation but would go uncovered.[30]

Third, while most officials who were entitled to absolute immunity were subject to other checks to prevent abuse of authority from going unredressed, similar built-in restraints in the name of national security did not exist.[31] The Court recognized the importance of national security activities to the safety of the country and its democratic system of government, but also noted that history abundantly documented government's tendency to view with suspicion those who dispute its policies.[32] Hence it concluded:

---

24. *Id.* at 513–15.
25. *Id.* at 520.
26. *Id.* at 521.
27. *Id.*
28. *Id.*
29. *Id.* at 521–22.
30. *Id.* at 522.
31. *Id.* at 522–23.
32. *Id.* at 523.

The danger that high federal officials will disregard constitutional rights in their zeal to protect national security is sufficiently real to counsel against affording such officials an absolute immunity.... We do not believe that the security of the Republic will be threatened if its Attorney General is given incentives to abide by clearly established law.[33]

In *Anderson v. Creighton*, the Supreme Court affirmed its decisions in *Harlow* and *Mitchell*, this time in a suit brought against an agent of the Federal Bureau of Investigation (FBI), who claimed entitlement to qualified immunity.[34] The Court pointed out that the relevant objective question in granting an FBI agent qualified immunity was whether a reasonable officer could have believed that the warrantless search was lawful in the light of clearly established law and the information which the searching officer possessed.[35] An officer who reasonably, albeit mistakenly, concluded he had probable cause should not be held personally liable.[36]

In another suit involving the FBI, *Wahad v. FBI*, a former Black Panther leader claimed that an FBI agent violated his rights of association and speech guaranteed by the First Amendment to the Constitution.[37] The federal agent argued he was entitled to qualified immunity because the law regarding the permissible limits of government conduct in interfering with the speech and association of groups such as the Black Panthers was not clear at the time, and he was only complying with FBI directives.[38] The court not only found that the constitutional rights of speech and assembly were clearly established, but it also held that obedience to internal orders did not entitle a federal official to qualified immunity.[39] The court said,

To allow one who obeys orders to escape liability for the direct violations of the constitutional rights of others would greatly narrow the effect of *Bivens*. The fact that one violates the constitutional rights of another because of the orders of superiors will not allow that person to avoid liability....[40]

---

33. *Id.* at 523–24.
34. *Anderson v. Creighton*, 483 U.S. 635, 640 (1987).
35. *Id.* at 641.
36. *Id.*
37. *Wahad v. FBI*, 813 F. Supp. 224 (S.D.N.Y. 1993).
38. *Id.* at 229.
39. *Id.* at 230.
40. *Id.*

C. Immunity, As Applied to U.S. Intelligence

The guidelines thus far established by Congress and the courts have not entirely settled the matter of when and who a private litigant can sue in the federal government. The immunity battle rages with particular fury when bringing a legal action for wrongdoing against government employees with intelligence functions, particularly the CIA's managing officials. Standing firmly entrenched in claims of national security and clinging to the vestiges of immunity, U.S. intelligence agencies try to place themselves beyond the reach of the law.

Nonetheless, given the Supreme Court's decision in *Mitchell v. Forsyth*, there is little likelihood that any intelligence official would be entitled to absolute immunity. Even the Director of the CIA, as the Attorney General, would be granted at most qualified immunity. In motions to dismiss, therefore, the CIA generally argues for qualified immunity, claiming that its Agency officials were performing a discretionary function and the law was not clearly established.[41] Qualified immunity means that an intelligence agency defendant could be liable for money damages to an injured party for violating clearly established constitutional or statutory laws.

Applying the *Anderson v. Creighton* standard in a suit against a CIA officer, the offending CIA officer might argue he made a mistake when he violated an individual's rights, but he acted in a way which he reasonably believed to be lawful. To convince the court he was entitled to qualified immunity, the defendant would have to demonstrate that a reasonable CIA officer would have believed his actions were lawful. The court would make its decision by examining both the existence of clearly established pertinent law and the information that the CIA officer possessed at the time he took the action which violated the individual's rights.

Obviously, pursuant to the court's decision in *Wahad v. FBI*, a claim by an intelligence officer that he was following the orders of his superiors when he violated a person's clearly established constitutional or statutory rights would not help in his defense. He would not be entitled to immunity for following orders.

In all cases against U.S. intelligence agencies and their officials, plaintiffs and counsel need to be prepared to counter arguments for immunity. They

---

41. In *Horn v. Albright*, CA 94-1756 (D.D.C 1994) (filed under seal in 1994), the lawyers for the CIA and the Department of State argued that it was not clearly established that the Fourth Amendment applied to U.S. citizens overseas.

must demonstrate that the Constitution and laws were clear and, therefore, that the defendants knew or reasonably should have known that their conduct would violate the plaintiff's rights and/or was not within their sphere of responsibility or authority. Basically, if intelligence agency defendants reasonably should have been aware that the action they took within their sphere of official responsibility would violate the constitutional or statutory rights of the plaintiff, immunity should not be available. The plaintiff's counsel should look to the statutes which Congress in its wisdom has passed and argue that the federal courts indeed have the authority to decide "*all* civil actions arising under the Constitution, laws, or treaties of the United States (emphasis added),"[42] including those against the U.S. Intelligence and its management.

---

42. 28 U.S.C. §1331 (West 1994).

CHAPTER THREE

CIA, As Exempted and Partially-Exempted Agency

Federal laws and regulations protect employees of most U.S. government agencies from illegal, adverse personnel actions taken against them by other government officials. Intelligence agency employees, particularly those working for the CIA, however, have many fewer administrative and judicial procedures available to them to redress employer abuse and wrongdoing. Exemptions given to the CIA under the national security rubric leave its employees largely unprotected.

The Civil Service Reform Act (CSRA), for example, provides protections and exclusive remedies for the majority of federal government civil servants who seek redress of employment-related grievances. The CIA is not covered by this Act. CIA lawyers, therefore, argue that by exempting the CIA from the CSRA, Congress intended to exclude CIA employees from protection against illegal and unfair employment actions, and, as a result, CIA employees have no protection or remedy. This controversial position is explored here.

The CIA also is exempted from the Whistleblower Protection Act, closing another potentially important avenue of protection from reprisals against the CIA whistleblower. The Administrative Procedure Act (APA), as well, does not protect the Agency employee from being terminated by the CIA Director under the nonreviewable authority vested in him pursuant to the National Security Act (NSA). These two exemptions also are discussed in this chapter.

U.S. intelligence agencies, including the CIA, however, are not exempt altogether from the APA. They can and have been sued under the Freedom of Information and Privacy Acts.

A. Civil Service Reform Act (CSRA)

The CSRA gives comprehensive, substantive protections against adverse personnel actions to most federal government employees.[1] For civil servants covered by this Act, the courts generally have held that Congress intended to make the CSRA their exclusive remedy for injuries arising out of an employment relationship. Those working for the CIA, however, are among the non-civil service federal employees to whom the CSRA's protections are unavailable. Thus CIA attorneys try to convince the court that in exempting certain federal government employees from the CSRA, Congress actually intended that these people have no redress. The following analysis looks to certain cases which have been brought in the federal courts and concludes that case law indicates non-civil service federal employees, including CIA officers, appear to have a right to turn to the courts to seek meaningful and adequate remedies for their causes of action.

1. CSRA — An Exclusive Remedy for Civil Servants

The CSRA created an elaborate framework for evaluating adverse personnel actions against federal officials.[2] The Act describes in great detail the protections and remedies applicable to civil servants, including the availability of administrative and judicial review. For the most part, it provides the exclusive remedy for civil servants.

The petitioner, in *Bush v. Lucas*, for example, was an employee of the National Aeronautics and Space Administration (NASA), which falls under the Civil Service Commission.[3] While his administrative appeal under the CSRA was pending, the petitioner filed an action in an Alabama state court, claiming a cause of action for damages under the First Amendment to the Constitution for retaliatory demotion. The suit eventually was removed to the federal system and finally reached the Supreme Court. The Supreme Court held that because the employee's claims arose out of "an employment relationship that is governed by comprehensive procedural and substantive provisions giv-

---

1. CSRA of 1978, Pub. L. No. 95-454, 92 Stat. 1111 (codified as amended in scattered sections of 5 U.S.C.).
2. *Lindahl v. OPM*, 470 U.S. 768, 774 (1985).
3. *Bush v. Lucas*, 462 U.S. 367 (1983).

ing meaningful remedies against the United States, it would be inappropriate for this Court to supplement that regulatory scheme with a new nonstatutory damages remedy."[4]

Similarly, in *Pinar v. Dole*, the defendant, a Federal Aviation Administration (FAA) police officer at Washington National Airport, brought suit against the Secretary of the Department of Transportation in her official capacity and against various employees of the FAA, in both their official and individual capacities, contesting three adverse personnel actions taken against him.[5] In this case, too, the court decided that procedures already in place under the CSRA were constitutionally adequate to protect Pinar's First Amendment interests. The court also held that the remedies provided under the CSRA were intended to be exclusive, and, thus, the court was not required to create a judicially-fashioned damage remedy.[6]

2. Unavailability of CSRA to CIA Employees

Unlike the civil service employees in *Bush* and *Pinar*, CIA employees are not part of the civil service system and are unable to take advantage of the substantive, in-depth protections of the CSRA which forbid arbitrary and illegal actions by supervisors and provide administrative and judicial procedures to redress wrongdoing. The CSRA, in fact, defines "agency" as an Executive Agency including the Veterans' Administration, the Library of Congress and the Government Printing Office, but specifically "does not include...the Central Intelligence Agency."[7] Moreover, the CIA has no functional or procedural equivalent to the CSRA. Unfortunately, there are no internal administrative remedies for CIA employees other than an inadequate grievance process managed by the CIA's Office of the Inspector General (OIG) and an Agency Office of Equal Employment Opportunity Office (OEEO). The officials of both entities are employed and paid by the CIA, are not independent or impartial, and have too often been part of the problem rather than the solution.[8]

---

4. *Id.*

5. *Pinar v. Dole*, 747 F.2d 899, 902 (4th Cir. 1984), *cert. denied*, 471 U.S. 1016 (1985).

6. *Id.* at 910.

7. *Am. Fed'n of Gov't Employees Local 3884 v. Fed. Labor Relations Auth.*, 930 F.2d 1315, 1319 n.4 (8th Cir. 1991); 5 U.S.C. §7103(a)(3)(C) (West 1996) (excludes CIA from definition of "agency").

8. *See* Chapter One, B.1.a. detailing the complicity of the Inspector General's Office. It provides examples of OIG collusion, retaliation and reprisals. These include the cases of:

3. Congressional Intentions in Exempting Non-Civil Service Federal Employees from CSRA

The question then arises whether or not Congress, by exempting non-civil service federal agencies, including the CIA, from the CSRA, intended that their employees have no external remedy for adverse personnel actions. Attorneys for a plaintiff-employee litigating against these agencies should be prepared to argue that our elected representatives indeed would not purposely leave non-civil service government employees without any protections or rights against their employers' abuses and/or wrongful conduct.

An important case addressing this issue was *Davis v. Passman.*[9] In *Passman,* the Supreme Court appears to have imposed a requirement that Congress, in legislating, must indicate explicitly its intent to displace judicially-created remedies. Here a former Congressional staffer brought suit alleging that the respondent, a United States Congressman, had discriminated against her on the basis of her sex by terminating her employment in violation of the Fifth Amendment. The lower court apparently interpreted section 717 of Title VII of the Civil Rights Act of 1964, 86 Stat. 111, 42 U.S.C. § 2000e-16, as a Congressional prohibition against judicial remedies for those in petitioner's position because, when section 717 was added to Title VII, it failed to extend its protection to Congressional employees.[10] The Supreme Court held, however, that there was no explicit declaration that Congress meant section 717 to foreclose alternative judicial remedies available to those unprotected by the statute. Such silence, the Court stated, was far from the "clearly discernible will of

---

Jill, case J, the woman who was the victim of an attempted rape and battery; Hannah, case H, the woman who was told she was too attractive and strong-willed to be sent to a certain overseas post; Doris, case E, the woman whose CIA employment was terminated because she wrote her elected representatives asking for help in redressing her grievances against the CIA; Thompson, case C, the woman Chief of Station (COS) who reported her deputy for alleged wife abuse; and, Ira, case I, the male COS who was relegated to a dead-end job outside of CIA headquarters to await retirement, after he reported information to the Director of the CIA alleging illegal activity on the part of the Inspector General. All of these individuals became targets of the OIG once they filed complaints or reported Agency wrongdoing. *See also* Chapter One, B.1.c. which provides case examples demonstrating OEEO's biases and prejudices against complainants. These cases demonstrate what confronts an employee who brings a grievance or complains.

9. *Davis v. Passman,* 442 U.S. 228, 246 (1979).
10. *Id.* at 247.

Congress."[11] Hence, the Court interpreted section 717 as leaving "undisturbed whatever remedies petitioner might otherwise possess."[12] It explained that were Congress to create equally effective alternative remedies, the need for damage relief might be obviated.[13]

In *Borrell v. United States International Communications Agency* (ICA), a former probationary employee of the ICA, not covered by the CSRA, brought a claim that she was wrongfully discharged in reprisal for blowing the whistle by reporting misconduct and abuse of authority.[14] The Court of Appeals addressed the issue whether Congress in passing the CSRA meant to take away from probationary employees preexisting rights of action to pursue constitutional claims in the federal courts. The government argued that the CSRA preempted alternative remedies, even those preexisting judicial remedies based upon the Constitution which had not been replaced by administrative appeals or judicial review of any kind.[15]

The Court of Appeals disagreed. As in *Passman*, the court held that where statutory remedies were unavailable to a particular segment of employees, Congress must make a clear statement indicating "explicitly its intent to displace judicially-created remedies for constitutional deprivations."[16] Where no such statement existed, the enactment of the CSRA did not revoke a probationary employee's preexisting right to seek redress of constitutional violations in district court. The court continued that it would be hard pressed to deny jurisdiction over a constitutional claim when the only alternative statutory remedy allowed no right of individual participation by the injured employee and permitted no judicial review of the merits of an agency's official decision not to investigate or prosecute an employee's claim.[17] Finally, the court ended with the assertion that it seemed clear that Congress intended the CSRA to provide additional, not decreased, protection for federal employees who report illegal or improper government conduct.[18]

In examining the issue of whether Congress, by exempting non-civil service federal employees from the CSRA, intended them to have no external ju-

---

11. *Id.*

12. *Id.*

13. *Id.* at 248.

14. *Borrell v. United States Int'l Communications Agency*, 221 U.S. App. D.C. 32 (1982); 682 F.2d 981, 983 (D.C. Cir. 1982).

15. *Id.* at 989, 990.

16. *Id.* at 989.

17. *Id.* at 990.

18. *Id.*

dicial remedy to redress wrongdoing, the *United States v. Fausto* decision and analysis become important.[19] Fausto, a nonpreference excepted service employee[20] in the Department of Interior Fish and Wildlife Service, brought a claim in federal court for wrongful discharge and back pay, after being told that under the CSRA an employee in his category had no right to appeal to the Merit Systems Protection Board. The Supreme Court denied his claim. The Court held that the comprehensive nature of CSRA, the Act's attention throughout to the rights of nonpreference excepted service employees, and the structure of the CSRA, combined to establish that its failure to include these employees in the provisions for administrative and judicial review of the type of adverse personnel action involved represented Congressional judgment that judicial review was unavailable.[21]

Specifically, the Court explained that the CSRA divided civil service employees into three main classifications generally described as senior executive service employees, competitive service employees and nonpreference excepted service personnel.[22] It pointed out that Congress failed to include nonpreference excepted service employees in provisions which afford other individuals in the civil service administrative and judicial review of personnel actions. The Court interpreted this failure to represent Congressional intent to foreclose review by nonpreference excepted service employees.[23]

4. Legal Precedent Indicating Non-Civil Service Federal Employees, Including Those Working for CIA, May Seek Redress in Courts

A number of cases have dealt with the question whether the CSRA preempts all alternative remedies for all federal government employees, including non-civil service federal employees, not covered and/or specifically exempted under the CSRA. Although the Supreme Court has not held on this particular issue, in *Bush* its explanation for deciding against the petitioner was that Bush already had meaningful, constitutionally adequate remedies.[24] Moreover, many lower courts which have addressed the issue prefer not to leave

---

19. *United States v. Fausto*, 484 U.S. 439 (1988).

20. A nonpreference excepted service employee within the CSRA is one who has not taken the competitive civil service examination.

21. *See supra* note 9, at 439–440.

22. *Id.* at 441.

23. *Id.* at 430, 440.

24. *See supra* note 3 at 368, 378.

non-civil service federal employees wholly unprotected. Thus, it would appear that intelligence agency employees, who have no CSRA protections and are not included in the Act, should not be precluded from availing themselves of the courts to redress alleged illegal, adverse personnel actions by other intelligence officials.

a. Lower Courts' Interpretation of Fausto

In *Matias v. United States*, the government tried to argue *Fausto*, claiming the CSRA's non-inclusion of certain categories of people in its provisions for administrative and judicial review established a Congressional judgment that those employees should not be able to demand judicial review.[25] Matias, a former enlisted man excepted from the CSRA, brought a complaint in the Claims Court under the Tucker Act in an effort to obtain both a correction of his military records by voiding his court-martial and an award of back pay for wrongful discharge.[26] The Court of Appeals supported Matias, concluding that the Claims Court properly exercised its jurisdiction to hear the plaintiff's collateral attack on his court-martial.[27] It specifically declined the government's "invitation to read a Fausto effect into this case."[28] *Matias*, therefore, lends support to the argument that the CSRA does not foreclose the possibility of non-civil service federal employees seeking legal redress in the federal courts.

A year later, in *Bosco v. United States*, the United States Court of Appeals in a rehearing *en banc*, interpreted Congressional silence as a deliberate Congressional choice to preserve what it did not explicitly take away.[29] Here again, the court rejected the government's argument that *Fausto* required the CSRA to provide the sole review procedures for any personnel actions involving federal government employees.[30]

Bosco and other federal employees had brought this suit to challenge the legality of the reclassification by the Internal Revenue Service of their positions from the "Prevailing Rate" (PR) system to the General Schedule (GS), whereby they lost grade and pay retention benefits.[31] Pursuant to the Tucker Act, the Claims Court had jurisdiction over a suit under the "Prevailing Rate"

---

25. *Matias v. United States*, 923 F.2d 821, 825 (Fed. Cir. 1990).
26. *Id.* at 822.
27. *Id.* at 825.
28. *Id.*
29. *Bosco v. United States*, 976 F.2d 710, 714 (Fed. Cir. 1992), *reh'g en banc.*
30. *Id.* at 711.
31. *Id.*

wage legislation (PR Act).[32] The government argued that the CSRA foreclosed all other remedies, pointing out the potential lack of consistency in decision-making without a single, comprehensive authority and complaining about the two layers of judicial review.[33]

In explaining its decision, the court noted that the implication of the government's position would not be limited to courts relying on Tucker Act jurisdiction, but would foreclose by implication all forms of judicial review (such as under the APA), thereby obliterating a cause of action under the PR Act.[34] The court continued, "We cannot sanction such violence to the PR Act without even a hint from Congress that it intended such changes...."[35] It suggested that any objections which the government had should be brought before Congress, noting the government had complained to the wrong forum.[36]

In 1993, in *Helsabeck v. United States*, a legal action by a non-appropriated fund instrumentalities (NAFIs) civilian food service director at a Marine air station was brought before a United States district court.[37] Here, a discharged employee claimed that his rights were violated when his Marine Corps employers did not follow proper procedures for terminating him. The plaintiff requested reinstatement to his former position, expungement of his personnel records and restitution for lost benefits.[38] The government, on the other hand, argued that judicial review of NAFI personnel decisions was not permitted because the CSRA specifically excluded NAFI employees.[39] It was the plaintiff's position, however, that the Administrative Procedure Act (APA) provided a basis independent of the CSRA for considering claims of wrongful discharge by NAFI employees.[40]

The court concluded that excluding NAFI personnel from the CSRA did not bar all judicial review for those employees because "it simply puts them outside the umbrella of CSRA protections."[41] Referring to *Fausto*, the court noted that purpose of the CSRA, as explained by the Supreme Court, was to provide an integrated scheme of administrative and judicial review designed

---

32. Prevailing Rate Act, Pub. L. No. 92-392, 86 Stat. 564 (1972) (codified as amended at 5 U.S.C. §§ 5341–49 (1988)).
33. *See supra* note 30, at 714.
34. *Id.*
35. *Id.*
36. *Id.*
37. *Helsabeck v. United States*, 821 F. Supp. 404 (E.D.N.C. 1993).
38. *Id.*
39. *Id.* at 405.
40. *Id.*
41. *Id.* at 406.

to balance a federal employee's legitimate interest with the needs of the administration.[42] The court explained that because NAFI employees were excluded from coverage of the Act, other remedies for wrongful termination, including the APA, could be available to them.[43]

The question then arises whether non-civil service federal government employees working for the CIA, who are not protected by the CSRA, are in Fausto's category, where judicial review is foreclosed. Unlike Fausto, who worked for the Department of Interior, or Bush and Pinar, NASA and FAA employees, respectively, CIA employees do not work for an agency encompassed by CSRA. Nor do they belong to any of the three main CSRA classifications—senior executive service employees, competitive service employees, or nonpreference excepted service personnel. They are not similarly situated to nonpreference excepted civil service employees whom, the Court determined in *Fausto*, Congress intended to exclude from review.

In *Fausto*, the Court looked to the CSRA's attention throughout to the rights of nonpreference excepted service employees and its comprehensive nature. It concluded that the Act's failure to include this category of employees in the CSRA's remedial scheme represented Congressional judgment that judicial review was unavailable.[44] On the other hand, the CSRA gives no similar attention, indeed no attention at all, to the rights of non-civil service CIA employees. Congress, in enacting the CSRA, did not appear to harbor any intentions whatsoever towards these exempted employees. The CSRA, therefore, should not necessarily be interpreted as purposely precluding CIA personnel from judicial review of adverse personnel actions in the courts of the U.S.

b. Conclusion

The Supreme Court has not yet spoken on the issue whether *Fausto* applies to non-civil service federal government employees not covered by the CSRA and specifically not included in the Act. The lower courts, however, have not been ready to accept arguments by government lawyers that, according to *Fausto*, the CSRA provides the only review procedures available to federal employees for adverse personnel actions and that by not including U.S. intelligence agencies, such as the CIA, within the CSRA scheme, Congress intended that their employees would not be entitled to judicial review. If lawyers for intelligence agencies insist that employees are precluded from seeking a remedy

---

42. *Id.*
43. *Id.*
44. *Id.* at 440, 441.

in the courts, the above cases represent judicial decisions to the contrary. Logically, it does not make sense that Congress would purposely intend to divest tens of thousands of government employees of their rights under other federal laws, which Congress itself has passed, or pursuant to the U.S. Constitution. Hence, counsel for intelligence agency plaintiffs should stand in a strong position regarding a *Fausto* argument.[45]

B. Whistleblower Protection Act

The CIA is exempt from the Whistleblower Protection Act (WPA) and the personnel practice constraints and prohibitions legislated under the Act.[46] The WPA specifically "does not include" the CIA or "any Executive Agency or unit thereof, the principal function of which is the conduct of foreign intelligence or counterintelligence activities."[47] Unfortunately, the Office of Special Counsel, established by the 1989 Act, has no provisions for dealing with classified information or for the authorization of disclosures of classified information, if necessary.

The CIA whistleblower, therefore, is not permitted to reap any benefits associated with the WPA and, in fact, has no similar independent, outside-the-CIA recourse or appeal. The CIA's non-inclusion in the WPA has allowed for unchecked reprisals by CIA management against those who report CIA wrongdoing.[48]

In recent years, after the CIA removed the security clearance of a Department of State officer for passing classified information to a member of the House Intelligence Committee about a CIA connection with a Latin American military officer allegedly involved in the murder of an American, members of the Senate acknowledged the need to protect CIA whistleblowers and suggested that CIA employees should be able to report Agency wrongdoing to them.[49] On March 9, 1998, the Senate approved a bill by a vote of 93 to one that would bar intelligence agencies, including the CIA, from punishing

---

45. *See also* Chapter Six, Section D which argues that the CSRA does not preclude non-civil service federal government employees, including those working for the CIA, from pursuing legal action in district court for violation(s) of their constitutional rights under *Bivens v. Six Unknown Fed. Narcotics Agents*, 403 U.S. 388 (1971).

46. WPA, Pub. L. No. 101-12, §3(i), 103 Stat. 16; 5 U.S.C. §1201 (1989).

47. 5 U.S.C. §2302(a)(2)(C)(i) (West 1996).

48. *See* Chapter One, Section B.

49. Walter Pincus, *CIA Official Rules for Blowing the Whistle*, Wash. Post, Mar. 31, 1998, at A3.

whistleblowers who provide to Congress classified information on the wrong-doings of their employers.[50]

To head off this legislation, the CIA's then-Inspector General (IG), Frederick Hitz, countered with an alternative proposal.[51] Hitz suggested that CIA whistleblowers first report Agency misconduct or wrongdoing to the OIG and then inform a member of the Congressional oversight committee.[52] The OIG would investigate the problem and provide the results to the DCI, the employee making the complaint, and the member of Congress who was privy to the report.[53]

As a result of the Senate's interest and the suggestions of Hitz, Congress included the "Intelligence Community Whistlerblower Protection Act of 1998," under the Intelligence Authorization Act of 1999. This Act acknowledged that:

> Congress, as a co-equal branch of the Government, is empowered by the Constitution to serve as a check on the executive branch; in that capacity, it has a "need to know" of allegations of wrongdoing within the executive branch, including allegations of wrongdoing in the Intelligence Community.[54]

but:

> the risk of reprisal perceived by employees and contractors of the Intelligence Community for reporting serious or flagrant problems to Congress may have impaired the flow of information needed by the intelligence committees to carry out oversight responsibilities[55]... [and] to encourage such reporting, an additional procedure should be established that provides a means for such employees...to report to Congress while safeguarding the classified information involved in such reporting.[56]

Included in this Act is an amendment of subsection (d) of section 17 of the Central Intelligence Agency Act of 1949 (50 U.S.C. §403(q)), where such a procedure is added. Unfortunately, because of the influence of the CIA's IG

---

50. *Senate Passes 'Whistleblowers' Protection,* Wash. Post, Mar. 10, 1998, at A6.

51. *See supra* note 48.

52. *Id.*

53. *Id.*

54. Intelligence Community Whistleblower Protection Act of 1998, Pub. L. No. 105-272, §701(b)(3), 112 Stat. 2397, 2413.

55. *Id.* at §701(b)(5).

56. *Id.* at §701(b)(6).

and the DCI, this procedure provides for the direct involvement and control of both the Agency's IG and the Director before any report is made to Congress. It specifies:

> An employee of the Agency, or a contractor to the Agency, who intends to report to Congress a complaint or information with respect to an urgent concern may report such complaint or information to the Inspector General (of the CIA). Not later than the end of the 14-calendar day period...the Inspector General shall determine whether the complaint or information appears credible. If...credible, the Inspector General shall, before the end of such period, transmit the complaint or information to the Director...[T]he Director shall, within 7 calendar days of such receipt, forward such transmittal to the intelligence committees, together with any comments...If the Inspector General does not transmit, or does not transmit in an accurate form, the complaint or information..., the employee...may submit the complaint or information to Congress by contacting either or both of the Intelligence committees directly....The employee may contact the intelligence committees directly...only if the employee—
>> before making such a contact, furnishes the Director, through the Inspector General, a statement of the employee's complaint or information and notice of the employee's intent to contact the intelligence committees directly; and obtains and follows from the Director, through the Inspector General, direction on how to contact the intelligence committees....
> The Inspector General shall notify any employee who reports a complaint or information to the Inspector General...of each action taken...with respect to the complaint or information. Such notice shall be provided not later than 3 days after any such action is taken. An action taken by the Director or the Inspector General under this paragraph shall not be subject to judicial review.[57]

Such internal or semi-internal whistleblower procedures for any government entity, particularly the CIA, generally are not workable because they subject employees to the exact risks of reprisal which the WPA is supposed to remedy. Given that the OIG, and sometimes the DCI, have been part of the problem for the CIA complainant, reporting wrongdoing first to the OIG could mean a disastrous end to the whistleblower's career. The procedures en-

---

57. *Id.* at § 702 (codified as amended at 50 U.S.C.A. § 403q(d) (West Supp. 2001)).

acted by Congress to protect the CIA whistleblower likely would have the opposite effect, placing control of the problem directly in the hands of the culprits. CIA retaliation against the individual probably would be inevitable.

C. Administrative Procedure Act— Partial Exemption

Freedom of Information and Privacy Acts—Not Exempt

The Administrative Procedure Act (APA)[58] is a durable, living and responsive law which has been used by federal employees to obtain equitable or injunctive relief for wrongful, adverse personnel actions.[59] In 1976, Congress amended the APA's judicial review provisions to eliminate sovereign immunity in suits against the government for remedies other than money damages.[60] As a result, the United States may be named as a defendant in such litigation. Now also included under the APA are the Freedom of Information Act (FOIA) and the Privacy Act.[61]

Exemptions from terms of the APA are not lightly to be presumed. Any modifications must be express.[62] The Air Force, for example, is specifically excepted from the APA's adjudicative procedures, although not apparently from FOIA.[63] U.S. Intelligence appears to be at least partially exempt in so far as security-related matters and the power of the Director of the CIA to fire CIA employees.

Suits against the CIA under the APA for claims other than those pursuant to the Freedom of Information and the Privacy Acts are relatively few. In 1983, a CIA employee filed a legal action against the CIA, alleging APA and constitutional violations.[64] Specifically, she claimed that the Agency's removal of her

---

58. APA, 5 U.S.C.A. § 551 *et seq.* (West 1996).

59. Alan B. Morrison, *The Administrative Procedure Act: A Living and Responsive Law*, 72 Va. L. Rev. 253, 268 (1986).

60. William H. Allen, *The Durability of the Administrative Procedure Act*, 72 Va. L. Rev. 235, 236 (1986); *see also* 5 U.S.C.A. §§ 701–03 and 710 (West 1996). Note: Sovereign immunity does not exclude claims for the equitable remedy of specific monetary relief such as back pay for work completed which is distinct from money damages.

61. APA, and amendments, 5 U.S.C. § 551 *et seq;* FOIA, 5 U.S.C. § 552; Privacy Act of 1974 (amended 5 U.S.C.A. § 552a (West 1996)).

62. 5 U.S.C.A. § 559 (West 1996).

63. 5 U.S.C.A. § 551, n.12 (West 1996).

64. *Doe v. CIA*, No. 83-3366, (D.D.C. Nov. 4, 1983). This case is different from *Thompson* filed over 10 years later, explained above as case C in Actual CIA Cases.

from a position as a covert staff member in the CIA's Directorate for Operations and its handling of her employee grievances were in violation of the CIA's own internal regulations. Her improper removal, she alleged, constituted action which was arbitrary, capricious and an abuse of discretion and was, therefore, unlawful under the Fifth Amendment and the APA.[65] The CIA settled this case the day it was scheduled to be heard in court, with no decision on either her APA or constitutional claims. Nevertheless, the case was settled in the plaintiff's favor.

Five years later in *Webster v. Doe*, the Supreme Court in part addressed the APA issue.[66] It held that the DCI's termination decisions under the section 102(c) of the National Security Act (NSA) authorizing termination,[67] when necessary or advisable in the interests of the United States, are not subject to judicial review under the APA.[68] In *Webster v. Doe*, a discharged Agency employee brought an action against the CIA's Director seeking declaratory and injunctive relief based on his claim that he was fired because of his admitted homosexuality. He alleged violations of the APA and of his constitutional rights. The Court denied his claim on the grounds that judicial review was precluded by virtue of the APA, since the CIA's action was committed to Agency discretion by the NSA.[69] Specifically, the Court wrote:

> it should be noted that section 102(c) allows termination of an Agency employee whenever the Director 'shall deem such termination necessary or advisable in the interests of the United States,' not simply when the dismissal is necessary or advisable to those interests. This standard fairly exudes deference to the Director, and appears to foreclose the application of any meaningful judicial standard of review.[70]

The Court noted, however:

> Subsection (a)(1) and (a)(2)...remove from judicial review *only* those determinations specifically identified by Congress or 'committed to Agency discretion by law' (emphasis added). Nothing in section 102(c) persuades us that Congress meant to preclude consideration

---

65. *Id.* at 22.
66. *Webster v. Doe*, 486 U.S. 592 (1988).
67. *See* National Security Act of 1947, ch. 343, §102(c), 61 Stat. 495, 498 (codified as amended at 50 U.S.C.A. §403-4(g) (West Supp. 2001)).
68. *See* 5 U.S.C.A. §701(a)(2) (West 1996).
69. *Supra note* 66.
70. *Id.* at 600.

of colorable constitutional claims arising out of the Director's action pursuant to that section. We believe that a constitutional claim based on an individual discharge may be reviewed by the District Court.[71]

Webster v. Doe's decision on the APA as it applied to the CIA was reaffirmed and extended by a lower court two years later in *Dubbs v. CIA*.[72] In *Dubbs*, the court held that the APA precluded review of the plaintiff's claim that the CIA violated its own directives set forth in DCID 1/14 (and Annex A) by focusing exclusively on her homosexuality and her homosexual conduct in denying her a Sensitive Compartmented Information (SCI) security clearance.

Dubbs argued that DCID 1/14 required the CIA to use the "whole person" concept in adjudicating SCI access application.[73] The court acknowledged the requirement for the "whole person" concept, but noted that the very first paragraph of DCID 1/14 stated, "The standards, procedures, and programs established herein are minimum and the departments and agencies may establish such additional security steps as may be deemed necessary and appropriate to ensure that effective security is maintained."[74] The court reasoned that the CIA, by allowing its officials to adopt whatever other actions they deemed "necessary," had not limited its discretion.[75] Further, the court pointed out that it was not in a position to determine whether any steps taken which deviated from the "whole person" concept were necessary to ensure that effective security was preserved, nor to decide whether granting Dubbs access to SCI would be clearly consistent with the interests of national security.[76] The court concluded that review of the plaintiff's claim was necessarily precluded by 5 U.S.C. 701(a)(2) (committing national security matters to CIA discretion by law), because there was no law to apply to this claim.[77]

It appears then that the APA closes off the possibility of judicial review of a plaintiff's claim when the DCI terminates an individual's employment with the Agency or the CIA refuses to grant or rescinds a security clearance. These national security-related actions were committed to CIA discretion by law.[78]

---

71. *Id.* at 603–604.

72. *Dubbs v. CIA*, 769 F. Supp 1113 (N.D. Cal. 1990).

73. *Id.* at 1120.

74. *Id.* at 1119.

75. *Id.* at 1120.

76. *Id.* at 1121.

77. *Id.*

78. Although the CIA, with its career propaganda and its career management and development and human resource offices, misleads its employees to believe they have careers with the CIA, in reality, they are at will employees, who, under the National Security Act

Nonetheless, other claims, such as those pursuant to *Bivens*,[79] alleging that CIA officers acting under the color of law deprived an employee of his or her constitutional rights, or those sounding in torts for wrongful termination may be reviewable by the courts, especially in view of the Supreme Court's comment in *Webster v. Doe* that nothing in the NSA precluded consideration of colorable constitutional claims arising out of the Director's action.[80] In this regard, a revoked security clearance or CIA employment would not be restored by the courts, but the plaintiff may be entitled to money damages.

In addition, all U.S. intelligence agencies, including the CIA, can be sued under FOIA and the Privacy Acts. Exhaustion of administrative remedies is a prerequisite for a civil action to compel an intelligence agency to amend its records under the Privacy Act.[81] Failure to exhaust, however, is not necessary if a plaintiff seeks money damages for an adverse Agency determination based on inaccurate records.[82] To state such a claim under the Privacy Act, a complainant must assert the required elements that:

(1) "the Agency acted in an manner which was willful and intentional,"[83]

(2) "[the Agency] fail[ed] to maintain any record concerning any individual with such accuracy, relevance, timeliness, and completeness as is necessary to assure fairness in any determination relating to the qualifications, character, rights, or opportunities of, or benefits to the individual that may be the basis of such record,"[84]

(3) "consequently a determination is made which is adverse to the individual,"[85]

(4) "[or an Agency] fail[ed] to comply with any other provisions of this section (5 U.S.C. §552a), or any rule promulgated thereunder, in such a way as to have an adverse effect on an individual,"[86] and

(5) as a direct and proximate result the individual suffered damages.[87]

---

of 1949, work at the discretion of the Director of Central Intelligence and can be fired at any time.

79. *Bivens*, 403 U.S. 388 (1971).

80. *See supra* note 66, at 593.

81. *Nagel v. HEW*, 725 F.2d 1439, 1441 (D.C. Cir. 1984).

82. *M.K. v. Tenet*, CA No. 99-0095, 99 F. Supp. 2d 12, 20 (D.D.C. Mar. 23, 2000) (*M.K. II*).

83. 5 U.S.C.A. §552a(g)(4) (West 1996).

84. *Id.* at §552a(g)(1)(C).

85. *Id.*

86. *Id.* at §552a(g)(1)(D).

87. *See supra* note 82, at 23.

Plaintiff's counsel also must heed the two-year statute of limitation period contained in the Privacy Act.[88] In a suit successfully brought under this section, the U.S. is liable to the individual in the amount equal to the sum of the actual damages and the costs of the action together with reasonable attorney fees.[89]

---

88. 5 U.S.C.A. §552a(g)(5) (West 1996); *Blazy v. Tenet*, 979 F. Supp. 10, 18 (D.D.C. 1997).
    89. 5 U.S.C.A. §552a(g)(4) (West 1996).

PART TWO

LEGAL REMEDIES

Although the problems in bringing a legal action against an intelligence agency are difficult and time-consuming, there are workable approaches which will maximize the prospects for a favorable outcome. The following chapters cover a number of possible legal remedies for discrimination, torts, constitutional violations, and civil conspiracies arising out of unlawful, adverse employment-related conduct undertaken by the U.S. government. The examination and analysis focus on Title VII, the Federal Tort Claims Act, *Bivens*, 42 U.S.C. § 1985, and RICO. A plaintiff's attorney in a suit against an intelligence agency also should consider, if appropriate, including Freedom of Information and Privacy Acts violations, discussed above in Chapter Three, Section C.

Legal action against the government based on violations of federal and/or state law and the Constitution may be pursued concurrently, depending on the facts and the strength of each infringement. As much as possible the counts should be separate and distinct, assert different interests, implicate different rights and address different harms, violations, and remedies. The complaint needs to provide an independent basis for each claim. A judge will be less likely to agree to a preclusion argument by the government if the counts do not appear to be a simple repackaging of the same claim.

In addition, lawyers for the plaintiff must keep a close eye on procedural matters. Missing the statute of limitations, naming the wrong defendant or failing to request a sum certain, when required, could provide the government a quick and easy ground for moving to dismiss a case.

The goal is to make the aggrieved person whole again. Realistically, attaining this objective is unlikely because employees who sue their agencies may well burn their bridges, destroy their careers or choose to resign even if they prevail. Relief for the plaintiff then may come in the form of a monetary award for damages and the payment of costs of the legal action and attorney fees rather than the resumption of a professional career. The employee should not expect an apology for wrongs done by an intelligence agency. It will not be forthcoming.

CHAPTER FOUR

TITLE VII OF CIVIL RIGHTS ACT OF 1964, EMPLOYMENT DISCRIMINATION

Heralded with optimism by some and repugnance by others, Title VII of the Civil Rights Act of 1964 brought to certain federally protected categories of people the hope of equality. This Act specifically prohibits employers from engaging in discrimination based on race, color, religion, sex or national origin.[1] Originally, Title VII did not specifically apply to federal government employees. Five years after it was passed, President Nixon ordered federal agencies to provide equal employment opportunity on the basis of merit and fitness and without discrimination.[2] It was not until 1972, however, that amendments to Title VII extended the protections of the Civil Rights Act of 1964 to federal government employees.[3] Individuals over 40 years of age similarly were given protection by the Federal Age Discrimination in Employment Act (ADEA). The ADEA allowed those past age 40 to bypass their own agency's internal employment discrimination mechanism and, after giving 30 days notice to the Equal Employment Opportunity Commission (EEOC), to pursue an age discrimination complaint by filing a civil action in a United States district court.[4] Finally, the Rehabilitation Act Amendments conferred Title VII rights and remedies upon disabled employees under programs receiving federal financial assistance or federal agencies.[5] The U.S. government, in fact, has the added responsibility to develop affirmative actions plans for its disabled employees.[6]

---

1. Title VII of the Civil Rights Act of 1964, 42 U.S.C.A. §2000e-2(a) (West 1994).
2. Exec. Order No. 11,478, 34 Fed. Reg. 12,985 (Aug. 8, 1969).
3. *See supra* note 1, at §2000e-16.
4. 29 C.F.R. §1614.201(a) (1999).
5. 29 U.S.C.A. §794 (West 1999); 29 U.S.C.A. §791 (West 1999), respectively.
6. 29 U.S.C.A. §791 (b) (West 1999).

All federal government agencies are bound by Title VII, including the CIA. The CIA, in fact, publishes a small booklet, "The EEO Process at a Glance," in which it acknowledges its responsibilities and legal obligations pursuant to Title VII.[7] Since employment discrimination is one area in which the CIA is not exempt, Agency employees in protected categories have sought refuge in Title VII, filing numerous complaints and civil actions against the CIA, to include a class action.[8]

In a straight Title VII suit, the plaintiff should expect that lawyers for the U.S. government first will move to dismiss the case or, in the alternative, request the court to grant summary judgment. The judges in the conservative District Court for the Eastern District of Virginia, where these employment discrimination cases against the CIA are heard, unfortunately concur all too often with such motions. If the case remains viable, however, the plaintiff has a good chance of a favorable settlement. The CIA rarely, if ever, will allow a case to reach the discovery phase. Rather than give up any information, the Agency generally chooses to settle.

This chapter on unlawful employment discrimination under Title VII covers various types of discriminatory treatment against individuals in federally protected categories. It begins with disparate treatment, the most obvious type of discrimination, and continues on to discuss sexual harassment. The courts have determined that under Title VII there are two types of unlawful employment harassment—quid pro quo and hostile work environment. Disparate impact then is examined, as well as the accompanying problems with and importance of statistics in disparate impact cases.[9] Each section considers burdens of proof and tests and criteria for establishing employment discrimination. Each part also applies the facts and analysis to U.S. intelligence agencies, particularly the CIA.

Following this substantive discussion of discrimination, there is an examination of the preclusionary effects of Title VII in multi-count suits and the legal arguments against preclusion. The plaintiff's attorney, when preparing a complaint encompassing Title VII and other statutory or constitutional violations, should anticipate the government's argument that Title VII precludes other counts. Hence, the pleading, where possible, should provide an independent basis for each count, distinguishing and separating harms and remedies.

---

7. U.S. Equal Employment Opportunity Comm'n, The EEO Process at a Glance 1 (2nd ed. 1995).

8. *Class action*, case D.

9. Disparate impact is a less obvious type of discrimination in which employment practices are facially neutral, but harm certain groups of employees, while disparate treatment means an employer treats one person or group less favorably than others based on race, color, religion, sex, or national origin.

A discussion of some procedural matters follows including timeliness, venue, and the preference for filing in district court rather than using the Equal Employment Opportunity Commission (EEOC) route. The chapter ends with a brief mention of damages and the right to a jury trial.

Discrimination

Section 703(a) of Title VII specifically spells out discriminatory and, therefore, unlawful employment practices. It provides:

> It shall be an unlawful employment practice for an employer—
> (1) to fail or refuse to hire or to discharge any individual, or otherwise to discriminate against any individual with respect to his compensation, terms, conditions, or privileges of employment, because of such individual's race, color, religion, sex, or national origin, or
> (2) to limit, segregate, or classify his employees or applicants for employment in any way which would deprive or tend to deprive any individual of employment opportunities or otherwise adversely affect his status as an employee, because of such individual's race, color, religion, sex, or national origin.[10]

A. Disparate Treatment

Disparate treatment may be the easiest type of employment discrimination to recognize. It is simply where an employer treats one person or group of people less favorably than others because of race, color, religion, gender or national origin. The plaintiff in a disparate treatment case must establish that similarly situated employees, not in a class protected under Title VII (for example, similarly situated white men), were not similarly treated. Undoubtedly, according to the Supreme Court, disparate treatment was the most obvious evil Congress had in mind when it enacted Title VII.[11]

---

10. *See supra* note 1.

11. *Int'l Bhd. of Teamsters v. United States*, 431 U.S. 324 (1977) is a good example of a disparate treatment case. In *Teamsters*, the company was accused of regularly and purposefully treating persons of color and Hispanic-surnamed Americans less favorably than Caucasians. The disparity in treatment allegedly involved the refusal to recruit, hire, transfer or promote minorities on an equal basis with white people. The Court decided ultimately that the only factual issues were whether there was indeed such a pattern and practice of disparate treatment and, if so, whether the differences were premised on race. In *Teamsters*, the Court found a systematic pattern and practice of discrimination against certain truckers in federally protected categories.

To prove a case alleging disparate treatment against the government, the allocation of burdens generally moves from the plaintiff to the defendant and then back to the plaintiff.[12] First, the complainant has the burden of proving by a preponderance of the evidence a prima facie case for discrimination. If this is accomplished, the burden of production shifts to the government, which must articulate a legitimate, non-discriminatory reason for its action.[13] Should the employer meet this burden, the plaintiff, in order to prevail, must prove again by the preponderance of evidence that the defendant's articulated reason for its actions was a pretext for discrimination.

Generally disparate treatment is subtle and invidious and, therefore, difficult to prove. Within the closed doors U.S. intelligence agencies, discrimination can be expected to be even more obfuscated and labyrinthine. In addition, these agencies use pretext, cover, clandestinity and evasion to obstruct the processing of claims against them. Nonetheless, the basic requirements for a disparate treatment case, whether against the CIA, another U.S. government agency or a business, are similar, and the plaintiff should proceed according to the guidelines established in EEOC Management Directive-110.

1. Disparate Treatment Exceptions and U.S. Intelligence

Two disparate treatment exceptions to Title VII are particularly applicable to U.S. intelligence agencies—the bona fide occupational qualification (BFOQ) exception and the national security exception. A BFOQ exempts a position from Title VII because that particular job requires a person of a certain religion, national origin or sex. This requirement is very difficult to prove, and the intelligence agency employee may well prevail if the discrimination is based on an ostensible BFOQ. In matters of national security, however, the plaintiff generally loses especially if hiring, employment, or re-employment is the issue. The plaintiff, however, could be entitled to money damages if his or her employment was terminated for discriminatory reasons in violation of Title VII or the Constitution.

a. BFOQ Exception

Pursuant to section 703(e) of Title VII, the EEOC may exempt a position from Title VII or the ADEA, if it establishes there is a BFOQ required for the

---

12. *Texas Dep't of Cmty. Affairs v. Burdine*, 450 U.S. 248 (1981).
13. *Id.* at 253.

performance of the duties of that position. This exception to the prohibition against disparate treatment in the employment setting applies only to religious, gender, age, and ethnic employment discrimination, not to discrimination based on race or color.[14]

The BFOQ exception means that an intelligence agency, in sending only men to assume certain high level positions in Latin America, Southeast Asia, or the Middle East, may argue there is a BFOQ for a male in these positions and places. A U.S. intelligence agency, particularly the CIA, could claim that foreign officials from these areas would not feel comfortable and might even be offended by working with women because their mores, customs and attitudes create obstacles to professional relationships with women. Consequently, the CIA might allege that women officers would jeopardize the CIA's foreign operations in certain countries. A U.S. intelligence agency generally would not succeed in this type of argument.[15]

The BFOQ analysis is quite straightforward. Building on a decision of the Fifth Circuit Court in *Weeks v. Southern Bell Telephone & Telegraph Co.*, the same court in *Diaz v. Pan American World Airways* identified a two-step BFOQ test.[16] First, the employer must establish that the particular job in question requires that the employee be only of a particular gender, religion, age, or national origin. For example, the employer needs to demonstrate that one gender is so essential to job performance that a member of the opposite sex could not do the same job. Second, the requirement must be reasonably necessary to the essence of the employer's business. Here the employer must show that a particular gender, religion, age or national origin is so important to the essence of the business operation that the business would be undermined if other employees were hired.[17] *Diaz*'s "essence of business" rule has since been adopted by all circuits which have considered the question of a BFOQ.[18] Gender, religion, age or national origin must be a necessity, not a convenience, and these aspects of the job must predominate.[19]

---

14. *See supra* note 1, at §2000e-2(e).

15. *See Fernandez v. Wynn Oil Co.,* 20 Fair Empl. Prac. Cas. (BNA) 1161 (C.D. Cal. 1979), for one case where a court actually approved of restricting the position of international marketing director to men.

16. *Weeks v. S. Bell Tel. and Tel. Co.,* 408 F.2d 228 (5th Cir. 1969); *Diaz v. Pan Am. World Airways, Inc.,* 442 F.2d 385 (5th Cir. 1971).

17. *Diaz v. Pan Am. World Airways, Inc.,* 442 F.2d 385 (5th Cir. 1971).

18. Herman H. Kay, *Sex-Based Discrimination,* 603 (3d ed., West Publishing Co. 1988).

19. *Id.* at 604.

Speaking for the Supreme Court, Justice Blackmun explained that the BFOQ requirement is a more stringent standard than a business necessity defense.[20] In *International Union v. Johnson Controls, Inc.*, the defendant had adopted a policy where all women, except those whose infertility was medically documented, were barred from jobs involving potential lead exposure exceeding the standard established by the Occupational Safety and Health Administration. The policy was not neutral in that it did not apply to male employees, despite evidence that lead exposure on the male reproductive system also had debilitating effects.[21] The Court examined both the language of the BFOQ provision of Title VII, which allows an employer to discriminate on the basis of gender "in those certain instances where...sex...is a BFOQ reasonably necessary to the normal operation of that particular business,"[22] and the Pregnancy Discrimination Act amendment to Title VII, which specifies that unless pregnant women differ in their ability to work, they must be treated the same as other employees.[23] It noted that these provisions prohibit an employer from discriminating against women because they are able to become pregnant, unless their reproductive potential prevents them from performing their job responsibilities.[24] The employer must direct its concerns to those aspects of the woman's job-related activities that fall within the essence of the particular business. The Court concluded that the respondent could not establish a BFOQ and that its policy was facially discriminatory.[25]

Clearly the BFOQ exception is very difficult for an employer to establish. It generally is limited to instances where gender, religion, age, or national origin interferes with the employee's ability to perform the job.[26]

Although throughout its many years of existence the CIA has maintained the myth that women are unable to serve in certain job capacities, in view of the stringent requirements for establishing a BFOQ exception, it is doubtful that many positions within any intelligence agency, including the CIA, would qualify. Nonetheless, intelligence agencies could argue with some degree of credibility that in certain Islamic countries which curtail women's activities, for instance, where only men are permitted to drive automobiles, women would not have the same access or relationships as men. Their gender, therefore, in-

---

20. *Int'l Union v. Johnson Controls, Inc.*, 499 U.S. 187, 188 (1991).
21. *Id.*
22. *See supra* note 1, at § 2000e-2(e).
23. *See supra* note 20.
24. *Id.*
25. *Id.*
26. *Id.*

terferes with their ability to perform their job, not because of any discriminatory policy, but because of another country's laws, customs, and mores.

b. National Security Exception

Title VII has a national security exception, section 703(g), which states:

> [I]t shall not be an unlawful employment practice for an employer to fail or refuse to hire and employ any individual for any position, (or) for an employer to discharge any individual from any position...if—
> (1) the occupancy of such position, or access to the premises in or upon which any part of the duties of such position is performed or is to be performed, is subject to any requirement imposed in the interest of the national security of the United States under any security program in effect...; and
> (2) such individual has not fulfilled or has ceased to fulfill that requirement.[27]

As a result of such an exception, government agencies involved in national security may be able to escape the consequences of unlawful employment discrimination by claiming that a security consideration was the reason for an adverse employment action.[28] For example, the Court of Appeals for the Fifth Circuit dismissed the case of former Federal Bureau of Investigation (FBI) agent Fernando Mata, concluding it lacked subject matter jurisdiction to review his claim.[29] In this case, the FBI revoked Mata's security clearance after he participated in a class action lawsuit against the FBI on behalf of present and former Hispanic employees. Mata's employment with the FBI required a security clearance and, therefore, the revocation of his clearance was tantamount to firing him. Mata sued, seeking relief under Title VII alleging retaliation for his participation in the class action. In its decision the court admitted sympathizing with Mata but, nonetheless, refused to assist him.[30] The opinion said:

> Because the court would have to examine the legitimacy and the possibly pretextual nature of the FBI's proffered reasons for revoking the employee's security clearance, any Title VII challenge to the revocation would of necessity require some judicial scrutiny of the merits

---

27. See *supra* note 1, at § 2000e-2(g).
28. *Perez v. FBI*, 71 F.3d 513 (5th Cir. 1995).
29. *Id.* at 513, 514.
30. *Id.*

of the revocation decision. As the Supreme Court and several circuit courts have held that such scrutiny is an impermissible intrusion by the Judicial Branch into the authority of the Executive Branch over matters of national security, neither we nor the district court have jurisdiction to consider those matters.[31]

Footnote six of this decision added,

We also understand the concern of federal agents, whose employment is conditioned on security clearances, that the lack of judicial review creates the potential for abuse by the agencies and bureaus employing them. This result, however, is required by the fact that security clearance determinations are…entrusted by law to the Executive.[32]

Unfortunately, this decision demonstrates the courts' unwillingness to review intelligence agencies' decisions or to grant or revoke security clearances even if the action was taken for unlawful discriminatory reasons. Hence, discrimination through the exploitation of security issues could continue with impunity.

There is evidence, in fact, that this type of discrimination may be on the increase. On April 9, 1999, Nina Totenberg, National Public Radio's (NPR) Legal Affairs Correspondent, reported that a young Jewish lawyer at the CIA had his security clearance revoked and had been placed on administrative leave without pay because of what appeared to be an unfounded suspicion of his dual loyalty with Israel, as well as his family's donations to the United Jewish Appeal and purchase of Israeli savings bonds. Totenberg explained that suspicion of the CIA lawyer was raised by another government agency, but one senior intelligence source, not in the CIA, told NPR that the information was not considered reliable, even by the FBI. According to Totenberg, Neal Sher, the young man's lawyer and one-time head of the Department of Justice's Nazi hunting section, decried the CIA's disparate treatment of religious Jews in security clearance matters which Sher said, "stood my hair on end."

Totenberg added that the government's security apparatus had produced a number of similar cases, including a Jewish Department of State officer whose non-Jewish lawyer expressed amazement by the clearly different screen used to evaluate Jews. Totenberg also mentioned a Jewish FBI counterintelligence agent who won a six-figure settlement and a lifetime annuity because she was suspended after a trip to Israel, which she had reported and received permission to take.

---

31. *Id.* at 514–15.
32. *Id.* at note 6.

Alleged disparate treatment by the Department of Energy concerning Chinese employees in positions requiring security clearances also has received heavy media coverage. According to an August 18, 1999 article in the "Washington Post," for example, the former chief of counterintelligence at Los Alamos National Laboratory admitted that there was not a shred of evidence against Chinese physicist Wen Ho-lee, who was fired in March 1999 on suspicion that he leaked nuclear secrets to China. The counterintelligence chief said that the Department of Energy's Office of Counterintelligence identified the physicist as the prime suspect because he was a Chinese-American. This "Washington Post" article quoted the counterintelligence chief, "there was nothing there—it was built on thin air."

Given the Judicial Branch's reluctance to review national security decisions taken by government agencies and Title VII's national security exception, a suit against an intelligence agency involving a security issue might best be brought pursuant to a constitutional violation, as well as to Title VII. The Supreme Court in *Webster v. Doe*, while finding unreviewable the Director of the CIA's discretionary power to fire an employee, noted that judicial consideration of colorable constitutional claims was not precluded.[33] In view of the Court's opinion, the Jewish lawyer at the CIA, who believes religion to be the reason for the adverse personnel action taken against him, may well have grounds for a legal action based on the denial of his constitutional right to freedom of religion, as well as to equal protection under the law. The focus of his complaint must not be on security considerations. The requested relief would be money damages, rather than employment or re-employment.

2. Conclusion

The requirements are the same in disparate treatment suits against all federal agencies, including the CIA. Regretfully, it may be more difficult to establish disparate treatment today when discrimination is more subtle than it was a decade ago. Reasonable sounding pretexts, other than discrimination, generally can be found for not giving an individual in a protected class a certain job, training or promotion. Despite the similarities of most disparate treatment cases, however, the burden on the plaintiff is greater in cases against intelligence agencies such as the CIA where records are secret, evidence is withheld, witnesses are not forthcoming and pretext, cover, secrecy and evasion are part of the business. If the plaintiff can counter the government's mo-

---

33. *Webster v. Doe*, 486 U.S. 592, 593 (1988).

tion for dismissal or summary judgment and bring the case to the discovery stage, he or she will have a good chance of a favorable settlement. The CIA would rather settle than give over the required information in discovery.

The two disparate treatment exceptions—national security and BFOQ—are uniquely applicable to intelligence agencies. In a discrimination suit involving the termination of employment or the refusal to hire on the basis of security, the plaintiff suing an intelligence agency likely will lose under the national security exception to Title VII. He or she, however, may have a greater chance of success where the action can be brought for a constitutional violation rather than for a discriminatory national security decision. If an intelligence agency decides, however, that being a male, a U.S.-born citizen, or a certain religion is a job qualification, it may find such a requirement highly difficult to prove. Hence the plaintiff's attorneys generally should be able to defeat a BFOQ exception.

B. Sexual Harassment

In 1986, the Supreme Court confirmed in *Meritor Savings Bank, FSB v. Vinson* that sexual harassment was indeed a form of discrimination.[34] Justice Rehnquist said, "Without question, when a supervisor sexually harasses a subordinate because of the subordinate's sex, that supervisor 'discriminates' on the basis of sex."[35]

This seminal sexual harassment case concerned a woman, Mechelle Vinson, who worked at a bank for four years during which time she made good advancement. It was undisputed that her advancement was based on merit. Shortly after assuming her teller-trainee job, however, her supervisor invited her to dinner and during that meal asked her to go to a motel with him for sex. Initially, she refused but, fearing she would lose her job, later relented. Over the course of the next few years, the supervisor repeatedly demanded sexual favors from Vinson both during and after business hours. He fondled her, followed her into the women's restroom, exposed himself to her and even forcibly raped her on several occasions.[36] Vinson testified that because of fear of her harasser, she never reported him to higher level bank managers or used the bank's complaints procedures. Vinson's supervisor denied all allegations.

---

34. *Meritor Sav. Bank, FSB v. Vinson*, 477 U.S. 57, 64 (1986).
35. *Id.*
36. *Id.* at 60.

The Supreme Court, in *Vinson,* held that sexual harassment was not only a barrier to women and minorities, but also created a hostile work environment which was a form of discrimination actionable under Title VII. The Court allowed that the language of Title VII was not limited to tangible or economic discrimination.[37] The wording "terms, conditions, or privileges of employment"[38] evinced a Congressional intent to eliminate the entire spectrum of discrimination in the workplace.[39] The Court recognized two types of sexual harassment—the quid pro quo and the hostile work environment—as furnishing legal grounds for an action pursuant to Title VII. Quid pro quo sexual harassment was based on sex in exchange for career advancement. Harassment, however, to be discriminatory may be, but does not have to be, directly linked to the grant or denial of an economic quid pro quo, as long as it unreasonably interferes with work performance or creates a hostile or offensive working environment.[40] "Title VII affords employees the right to work in an environment free from discriminatory intimidation, ridicule, and insult."[41]

The Supreme Court also found that the alleged voluntariness of the sexual relationship, in the sense that plaintiff was not forced to participate against her will, was not a defense to a sexual harassment claim brought under Title VII.[42] The "gravamen of any sexual harassment claim is that the alleged sexual advances were 'unwelcome.'"[43] The inquiry must be whether Vinson's conduct indicated her supervisor's advances were unwelcome, not whether her actual participation was voluntary.[44]

In *Vinson,* the Supreme Court declined to issue a definitive ruling on employer liability, but it agreed with the EEOC that Congress wanted the courts to look to agency principles for guidance.[45] The Court noted, however, that Congress' decision to define "employer" to include any "agent" of an employer demonstrates an intent to place some limits on acts of employees for which employers may be held responsible under Title VII.[46] The absence of notice to an employer, the fact an employee does not report the harassment or file a

---

37. *Id.* at 64.
38. *See supra* note 1, at §2000e-2(a)(1).
39. *Meritor Sav. Bank, FSB v. Vinson,* 477 U.S. 57, 60 (1986).
40. *Id.* at 65.
41. *Id.*
42. *Id.* at 68.
43. *Id.*
44. *Id.*
45. *Id.* at 72.
46. *Id.*

complaint, does not necessarily insulate the employer from liability, according to *Vinson*.[47]

Although *Vinson* found that for sexual harassment to be actionable, it must be sufficiently severe or pervasive to change the conditions of employment and create an abusive working environment,[48] it was not until 1993 in *Harris v. Forklift Systems, Inc.*, that the standards for a hostile environment were more clearly defined by the Supreme Court.[49] The claim in *Harris* was that the company's president insulted Harris because of her gender and frequently made her the target of unwanted sexual innuendoes. Harris complained and the president promised to stop but, in fact, did not. Since the president's harassment did not seriously affect Harris' psychological well-being or cause her to suffer injury, however, the question before the Court was to define what conduct was sufficiently severe or pervasive to create a hostile work environment.[50]

In its decision, the Court identified some boundaries to an adverse work environment actionable under Title VII. It found both an objective element and a subjective element were needed to meet the test for an abusive or hostile working environment. The standard required an objectively hostile environment, as well as the victim's subjective perception that the environment was abusive.[51] The Court said that as long as the environment would reasonably be perceived, and is perceived, as hostile, there was no need for a psychological injury.[52] Whether the environment was sufficiently adverse to be actionable under Title VII could be determined by examining not a single factor, but all the circumstances, such as the frequency and severity of the discriminatory conduct and whether it was humiliating or physically threatening or it unreasonably interfered with work performance.[53]

1. Sexual Harassment and U.S. Intelligence

Sexual harassment has been a problem for some federally-protected categories of employees working at U.S. intelligence agencies, particularly the CIA. Despite regulations and policies prohibiting such harassment, it seems to be

---

47. *Id.*
48. *Id.* at 67.
49. *Harris v. Forklift Sys., Inc.*, 510 U.S. 17 (1993).
50. *Id.* at 21.
51. *Id.* at 17.
52. *Id.* at 22.
53. *Id.* at 23.

continuing within the CIA. Sexual harassment occurs in a relatively unhampered fashion because the CIA's mechanisms for handling such problems simply do not work.

Victims of sexual harassment in the CIA generally do not report their harassers for fear of what would happen to them should they dare to speak out. The CIA's unclassified "Glass Ceiling" study under "Adverse Work Environment" noted a "pervasive fear of reprisal that inhibits employees from lodging complaints."[54] In addition, the "Executive Summary" of that "Glass Ceiling" report stated:

> A substantial number of women and minorities indicated that the working environment was uncomfortable and alienating. Although the number of formal and informal complaints reported for sexual or racial harassment is remarkably small, the incidence of sexual or racial harassment reported in the interviews, focus groups and the survey was substantial (between one-third and one-half of the women in every racial group reported having experienced some sexual harassment; racial harassment also was reported as prevalent, particularly for Blacks). Because harassment creates feelings of inferiority and powerlessness in those who are harassed, it serves as a barrier to women and minorities at the Agency.[55]

These statements clearly demonstrate that the CIA's complaints mechanisms are ineffective.[56] *Vinson* indicated that although an employer has a mechanism in place to report sexual or racial harassment, it still may be held liable for unlawful discrimination. If the victims of harassment are afraid to avail themselves of internal complaint procedures, the employer could be deemed responsible.

2. Conclusion

A female employee of an intelligence agency claiming sexual harassment may have an actionable case under Title VII if: (a) she were asked for sexual favors in return for a career advancement, whether or not she agreed, or (b) if she were subjected to a hostile work environment based on gender. Similarly, racial harassment at an intelligence agency could take the form of a quid

---

54. Prof'l Res. Inc. & Hubbard & Revo-Cohen, Inc., "CIA, Glass Ceiling Study" at 5 (1992).
55. *Id.* at 3.
56. *Id.*

pro quo or an abusive working environment for the minority employee.[57] To meet the test of a hostile environment, the harassment must be sufficiently pervasive and severe to change the conditions of employment. The victim, as well as a reasonable person, must look at all the circumstances and perceive the employment situation as hostile.

A plaintiff, where possible, should save the evidence of sexual advances such as notes, letters or messages left on an answering machine. Innuendoes, comments and insults which contribute to an abusive working environment may well be overheard by other employees. Even reluctant witnesses can be subpoenaed in a suit against the CIA, and every employee will not lie about such misconduct. Nonetheless, in the CIA environment of cover, cover up, pretext, evasion, secrecy and old boys, needed information, evidence and witnesses may be hard to come by.

C. Disparate Impact

This section examines disparate impact—employment practices that are facially neutral but, in fact, fall more harshly on one group than another and cannot be justified by business necessity. It explains the objective and subjective components of disparate impact and discusses the importance of statistics. Disparate impact is less obvious than disparate treatment and thus may be more difficult to recognize. A discriminatory motive, however, is not necessary to prove a disparate impact case.[58]

Lawyers involved in a disparate impact case against an intelligence agency probably would require statistical data to prevail. Problems in obtaining statistics may include the agency's refusal to grant access to needed information, high costs and time constraints, conflicting interpretations and analyses of the data and the possible misuse and abuse of the statistics by the intelligence agency.

1. Fair in Form, Discriminatory in Operation

Griggs v. Duke Power Co. was a precedential disparate impact case against a company which exploited testing as a pretext for discrimination.[59] In *Griggs,*

---

57. *Doris,* case E, a foreign born Black woman appears to have been subjected to a hostile work environment at the CIA based on her race and national origin.

58. *See supra* note 1.

59. *Griggs v. Duke Power Co.,* 401 U.S. 424, 427 (1971).

the defendants worked for a business that had five departments, only one of which, the labor department, employed people of color. In the labor department the highest paying jobs paid less than the lowest paying jobs in the other four more desirable departments. To qualify for placement in any department other than labor, it was necessary to score satisfactorily on two tests, neither of which was intended to measure the ability to perform a particular job or category of jobs.[60]

The Supreme Court held this practice violated Title VII. It explained:

> Under the Act, practices, procedures, or tests, neutral on their face, and even neutral in terms of intent, cannot be maintained if they operate to "freeze" the status quo of prior discriminatory employment practices.… What is required by Congress is the removal of artificial, arbitrary, and unnecessary barriers to employment when the barriers operate invidiously to discriminate on the basis of racial or other impermissible classification.… The Act proscribes not only overt discrimination but also practices that are fair in form, but discriminatory in operation.… If an employment practice which operates to exclude Negroes cannot be shown to be related to job performance, the practice is prohibited.[61]

Moreover, the Court did not believe that good intent or the absence of discriminatory intent would redeem employment procedures that operated against protected groups and were unrelated to job performance or capability.[62] The thrust of Title VII, it said, was directed toward the consequences of employment practices rather than the motive.[63] In a disparate impact case, it was the employer rather than the plaintiff that had the burden of demonstrating that its requirements and practices were business necessities.[64]

2. Objective and Subjective Components and Burdens of Proof

Many years later in *Atonio v. Wards Cove Packing, Co.*, the Ninth Circuit *en banc* further refined the disparate impact standards. It found disparate impact was not limited to objective criteria such as testing and academic degrees, but

---

60. *Id.* at 428.
61. *Id.* at 430 and 431.
62. *Id.* at 432.
63. *Id.*
64. *Id.*

could be applied to challenge subjective employer practices.[65] The court viewed employment practices from the perspective of their impact on the protected class and noted that almost all criteria necessarily have both objective and subjective components.[66]

Atonio also spelled out the three elements of the plaintiff's prima facie case. First, he or she must show a significant disparate impact on a protected class. Then the plaintiff must identify the specific employment practice or selection criterion, objective and/or subjective that is challenged. Last, the plaintiff needs to demonstrate a causal relationship between the practice and the impact.[67] Causation generally may be established by statistical evidence which is sufficiently significant or substantial to show that the practice in question has caused the exclusion of members of a protected class from jobs or promotions.[68]

After the plaintiff establishes his or her prima facie case for discrimination, the burden then shifts to the defendant to demonstrate that the challenged practice has a manifest relationship to the employment in question and is based on legitimate business reasons.[69] If this burden is met, the plaintiff then must show there are other tests or selection devices, without a similarly undesirable discriminatory effect, that would serve the employer's legitimate interests.[70]

In 1991, Congress also took an interest in the burden of proof in disparate impact suits. It amended the Civil Rights Act of 1964, setting forth two methods to substantiate a disparate impact claim and the responsibilities of the plaintiff and defendant in meeting their burdens of proof. Specifically, the plaintiff's burden in a disparate impact is established only if he or she:

> demonstrates that [an employer] uses a particular employment practice that causes a disparate impact on the basis of race, color, religion, sex, or national origin and the [employer] fails to demonstrate that the challenged practice is job related for the position in question and consistent with business necessity, or... [the plaintiff] makes the demonstration... with respect to an alternative employment practice and the [employer] refuses to adopt such alternative employment practice.[71]

---

65. *Atonio v. Wards Cove Packing Co.*, 810 F.2d 1477, 1482 (9th Cir. 1987) (*en banc*).
66. *Id.* at 1485.
67. *Id.* at 1482.
68. *Watson v. Fort Worth Bank & Trust*, 487 U.S. 977, 994 (1988).
69. *Id.* at 997.
70. *Id.* at 998.
71. The Civil Rights Act of 1964, as amended in 1991, explains that with respect to demonstrating that a particular employment practice causes a disparate impact, the com-

The employer then meets its burden of proof by showing a particular employment practice does not cause a disparate impact. Success in meeting this burden eliminates the need to demonstrate that the practice is a business necessity. If the employer is unable to demonstrate that the employment practice does not cause a disparate impact, the company then must show it is required as a business necessity. A business necessity excuse, however, is not a defense for intentional discrimination.[72]

The Supreme Court has concurred with the burden shifting requirements in *Atonio* and with its approach to subjective judgments of employers which could result in discrimination, whether or not intentional. In *Watson v. Fort Worth Bank and Trust*, the Court agreed with the lower courts that discretionary, subjective employment practices may be analyzed under the disparate impact approach in appropriate cases.[73]

Watson sued her former employer, the Fort Worth Bank, under Title VII, alleging the bank's practice of committing promotion decisions to the subjective discretion of supervisory employees led to illegal racial discrimination.[74] Here, as in many disparate impact cases, statistics were key. Watson's statistics evidenced that a woman of color who applied for a position with the bank had one-fourth the chance of a white applicant to obtain the job. If she were hired, her performance was apt to be evaluated 30 points lower than her white counterpart. She would be paid $46.00 per month less and be advanced at a rate six-tenths of a pay grade per year more slowly than a white person with the same qualifications.[75]

Using the disparate impact criteria, the Court determined that an employer's practice of committing promotion decisions to the subjective discretion of supervisory employees may result in illegal discrimination. It noted that the disparate impact analysis might effectively be abolished if an employer could insulate itself from liability simply by combining objective selection practices with a subjective component, such as a brief interview.[76] Allowing

---

plainant must show "each particular challenged employment practice causes a disparate impact." If, however, the complaining party establishes that "the elements of a respondent's decisionmaking process are not capable of separation for analysis, the decisionmaking process may be analyzed as one employment practice." *See supra* note 1, at § 2000e-2(k) (West 1994); Pub. L. No. 102-166, 105 Stat. 1071, 1074 (1991).

72. *Id.*
73. *See supra* note 70, at 991.
74. *Id.* at 981.
75. *See supra* note 20, at 586.
76. *See supra* note 70, at 977.

employers "to escape liability simply by articulating vague, inoffensive-sounding subjective criteria would disserve Title VII's goal of eradicating employment discrimination...."[77]

3. Disparate Impact and U.S. Intelligence

In the case of U.S. intelligence agencies, as with other employers which have a workforce numbering in the tens of thousands, statistics are very significant and valuable in proving disparate impact, particularly with regard to a class action. Even the meager statistics available on employment within the CIA, for example, indicate women in the CIA entering the junior officer training program have been as qualified as men hired for the same program, but the overwhelming majority entered on duty at lower grades.[78] In fact, according to the CIA's "Glass Ceiling" study, men start at a higher grade than women, and this difference increases as the age of new entrants increases.[79] Statistical analysis from the "Glass Ceiling" report indicates that promotion rates for the entire Agency, especially in the Clandestine Service, are higher for men than women and for whites in comparison to minorities.[80] As the years pass, the men progress to the highest ranks of the Agency, assuming most upper level management and Chief of Station positions, while the women hit the glass ceiling and remain at the lower level desk jobs.[81]

After the CIA's class action suit, the journeyman level for all operations officers in the Clandestine Service was raised to a GS-13, meaning most women and minority CIA officers will reach the grade of GS-13 before retirement.[82] Nonetheless, to the extent the male managers within the Clandestine Service still are able directly and indirectly to influence and control promotions and assignments, the situation appears to remain inequitable.

Facts and statistics are needed to substantiate a disparate impact claim against intelligence agencies. These agencies, however, stand behind secrecy

---

77. *Id.* at 980.

78. Findings from an internal CIA study conducted by the CIA's Directorate of Operations, "Working Group on Category B (case officers) Women Officers," Nov. 1992.

79. *See supra* note 54.

80. *Id.* at 2.

81. *Id.* at 1. The unclassified "Glass Ceiling" study found women concentrated in lower grades than men, and Black, Asians, Hispanics, and Native Americans concentrated in lower grade levels than Whites. It noted while women constituted nearly 40 percent of the professional workforce, women held only nine percent of the senior intelligence service positions.

82. *Class action*, case D.

and generally will not provide access to a plaintiff's statisticians. When the CIA finally was forced to give information to the statisticians for the class action, these experts found "significant disparities...to exist in the effect that certain employment policies have on women [operations] officers."[83] The discovery techniques that made this conclusion possible were not spelled out.

4. Conclusion

At best there may be disagreements and different interpretations of the statistics. A worse case scenario would be the actual misuse and abuse of statistics by intelligence agencies.[84]

The EEOC's "Uniform Guidelines on Employee Selection Procedures" provide some direction regarding problems with statistics.[85] The Guidelines adopted an enforcement rule under which adverse impact generally will not be inferred unless the members of a protected class are selected at a rate less than four-fifths of the rate at which the group with the highest rate is selected.[86] This standard has been criticized on technical grounds. As an alternative, courts sometimes use a standard deviation analysis. No consensus, however, has developed around any alternative mathematical standards. Courts, instead, generally judge the "significance" or "substantiality" of numerical disparities on a case-to-case basis.

Despite problems, obtaining valid statistical data is essential in a disparate impact action against intelligence agencies. Attorneys, therefore, must push hard to secure accurate statistics which may serve to be the critical piece of the puzzle and the key to winning a case.

D. Retaliation

Additional discrimination often derives from, accompanies and/or follows a Title VII complaint. In fact, in almost every, if not every, case mentioned above in the section on Actual CIA Cases, the complainant has filed retaliation/reprisal complaint(s) after initiating the original grievance. Retaliation in

---

83. *Conway v. Studeman*, C.A. No. 95-426A (E.D. Va. 9 June, 1995) (referring to Notice of Class Action, Proposed Settlement and Fairness Hearing).

84. *See supra* note 66, at 995 n.3.

85. EEOC "Uniform Guidelines on Employee Selection Procedures," 29 C.F.R. § 1607 (1987).

86. *Id.*

the CIA has taken the form of denial of assignments or promotions, poor performance evaluations, medical holds, investigations by the Office of the Inspector General, fitness for duty evaluations, Personnel Evaluation Board recommendations for termination of employment, Office of Security reinvestigations and polygraphs and sometimes personal threats and humiliation. Employees or managers, not wanting to become "splattered with mud,"[87] may turn a blind eye, acquiesce in, condone, ratify or endorse these actions. Reprisal and retaliation are such within the CIA that filing a grievance or complaint often means the end of the aggrieved party's career.

Retaliation is unlawful. Any and all such behavior is part and parcel of the discrimination and should be grieved and included in the plaintiff's complaint.[88]

To establish a prima facie case for retaliation, plaintiffs must demonstrate that: (1) they engaged in a protected activity such as filing a complaint for discrimination or participating in a discrimination proceeding; (2) the alleged retaliator knew of the protected activity; (3) they suffered an adverse employment action,[89] and (4) the protected activity and the adverse employment action were causally related.[90]

To succeed in a claim of retaliation, the plaintiffs need not prevail on the underlying claim of discrimination.[91] Employee-litigants must only establish that they were acting under a "good faith reasonable belief" that they were victims of unlawful discrimination.[92]

Moreover, the party asserting the claim of retaliation does not have to be the same person who suffered the discriminatory employment action.[93] According to EEOC Guidance, retaliation is prohibited against someone so closely associated with the complainant that the retaliation would discourage or prevent that person from participating in the discrimination proceedings.[94]

The Supreme Court has not yet addressed the issue of what an adverse employment action actually is. The majority of jurisdictions, however, have taken

---

87. The Inspector General of the CIA warned a ranking CIA official that he should not help Thompson, case C, lest he too become "spattered with mud."

88. See supra note 1, at § 2000e-3(a).

89. Glover v. South Carolina Law Enforcement Div., 170 F.3d 411, 413 (4th Cir. 1999), cert. denied, 528 U.S. 1146.

90. Id.

91. Eve Klein & Rosemary Halligan, A Rising Tide of Retaliation Claims Challenges Employers to Adopt Adequate Preventive Measures, N.Y. St. B.J., Sept.–Oct. 1999, at 51, 51–52.

92. Id. (See also Grant v. Hazelett Strip-Casting Corp., 880 F.2d 1564, 1569 (2d Cir. 1989)).

93. Id. at 53.

94. EEOC Guidance 8–9.

an expansive approach to what constitutes such actions.[95] Most courts which have considered the issue have held that section 704(a) of Title VII broadly prohibits an employer from retaliating against its employees in any manner for engaging in a protected action.[96]

In addition, EEOC Guidance criticizes as "unduly restrictive" those court decisions which have held that the retaliation provisions apply only to "ultimate employment actions" or even employment actions that "materially affect the terms, conditions, or privileges of employment."[97] The EEOC instead advocates that all "adverse treatment that is reasonably likely to deter protected activity" warrants protection under Title VII.[98]

Generally, circumstantial evidence is relied upon to establish unlawful retaliation.[99] The circumstantial evidence showing that the protected activity and the adverse action are linked frequently includes demonstrating that the adverse employment action occurred shortly after the protected activity and that the alleged retaliator was aware that the complainant had engaged in a protected activity.[100] If an employer's justification for the adverse action is comprised of several factors and its motivations are mixed, which is often the case, the controversy will be fact intensive and, at a minimum, the employer must prove that it would have taken the action notwithstanding its consideration of the discriminatory reasoning alleged.[101]

E. Discrimination As Continuing Violation

A complaint of discrimination as a continuing violation generally alleges a pattern of unlawful discrimination which has continued in a series of related acts of a similar nature or involves the same management. One or more of the

---

95. *See supra* note 91, at 54.

96. *Id. See also Wideman v. Wal-Mart Stores, Inc.,* 141 F.3d 1453, 1456 (11th Cir. 1998); *Torres v. Pisano,* 116 F.3d 625 (2d Cir. 1997); *Yerdon v. Henry,* 91 F.3d 370 (2d Cir. 1996); *Knox v. Indiana,* 93 F.3d 1327, 1334 (7th Cir. 1996); *Berry v. Stevinson Chevrolet,* 74 F.3d 980, 984-86 (10th Cir. 1996); *Wyatt v. City of Boston,* 35 F.3d 13, 15-16 (1st Cir. 1994); *Yartzoff v. Thomas,* 809 F.2d 1371, 1375 (9th Cir. 1987); *Vergara v. Bentsen,* 868 F. Supp. 581, 592 (S.D.N.Y. 1994); *Passer v. Am. Chem. Soc'y,* 935 F.2d 322, 331 (D.C. Cir. 1991).

97. EEOC Guidance at 8–11.

98. EEOC Guidance at 8–15.

99. *See supra* note 91, at 54.

100. *Id.*

101. *Id.*

discriminatory acts must fall within the limitations period. The aggrieved party needs to show that he or she suffered a present loss or harm with respect to a term, condition or privilege of employment for which there exists a remedy.[102] An old loss or harm will not suffice.

The CIA's Office of Equal Employment Opportunity (OEEO) can be expected to reject allegations of a pattern of discrimination that has continued over a period of time, refusing to investigate such complaints. The Agency will not even consider that it has unlawfully discriminated for years against certain individuals or groups of employees. A complainant alleging a continuous violation must appeal the rejection to the EEOC or the courts, or lose that cause of action. The appeal can only be initiated, however, after the CIA's OEEO issues a Final Agency Decision (FAD) on any other allegations which it has accepted for investigation. Since the CIA's OEEO generally takes about two years or more to issue a FAD, a plaintiff cannot even begin the appeal process of the CIA's rejection of a claim of discrimination as a continuing violation for at least two years.

Conway, case G, filed a complaint alleging discrimination as a continuing violation based on her national origin in a series of related discriminatory acts over a 20-year period. The CIA's OEEO rejected her timely complaint for failure to state a claim upon which relief could be granted because she had not demonstrated a present harm to the terms, conditions and privileges of her employment. Then it was able to dismiss all the remaining related allegations as untimely. Conway filed a civil action in the District Court for the Eastern District of Virginia in an attempt to obtain some justice. That conservative court concurred in the CIA's motions to dismiss without even giving Conway a hearing.

F. Preclusion

This section addresses the question whether a Title VII action forecloses a plaintiff's ability to maintain related or separate claims. It makes the argument and provides case law to indicate that Title VII is not necessarily preemptive, particularly of those claims against government officials in their individual capacities for violations of the Constitution and/or federal or state laws. Separate causes of actions, particularly counts for which Title VII provides no remedy, have been maintained concurrently with Title VII suits. Nonetheless, since the government routinely files motions arguing for preclusion even if employment

---

102. *Diaz v. Dep't of the Air Force*, EEOC Request No. 05931049 (Apr. 21, 1994).

discrimination is only part of the complaint, the plaintiff and counsel are cautioned to make their counts as separate and distinct as possible.

1. Government Tactics

If a multi-count complaint, which includes allegations of unlawful employment discrimination, is filed in district court against an intelligence agency and its officials, the government's first line of defense may be to argue that all claims other than Title VII must be dismissed on the grounds of preclusion.[103] In the *Thompson* case, for example, the government filed a motion requesting the court to dismiss Thompson's non-Title VII claims because Title VII provides the exclusive remedy for claims of employment discrimination.[104] To support its motion, the government relied on *Brown v. General Services Administration* as its seminal case.[105] It argued that the Supreme Court in *Brown* found that Title VII provided the sole judicial remedy for claims of discrimination in federal employment. According to *Brown*, the Civil Rights Act of 1964 created an "exclusive, preemptive administrative and judicial scheme for the redress of federal employment discrimination."[106]

2. Arguments against Preclusion

There is ample case law from which to argue that Title VII does not appear to foreclose other remedies. *Brown*, in fact, never addressed the question whether Title VII had any preemptive effect on claims brought against federal agents in their individual capacities for constitutional or statutory violations arising either from related or separate causes of action for which Title VII provided no relief.[107]

The year following *Brown*, the District Court in the District of Columbia, in *Brosnahan v. Eckerd*, addressed the question whether *Brown* immunized

---

103. *Thompson*, case C.

104. *Id.* The government's tactic appears to be: first, the CIA's OEEO decides against the employee in its Final Agency Decision, declaring there was no discrimination. According to an OEEO counselor who requested anonymity, the CIA's OEEO decides against the complainant in over 98 percent of the cases. The CIA's OEEO is supposed to file these statistics with EEOC annually. Second, if the complaint is filed in court, the government tries to persuade the court to dismiss all non-Title VII counts on the grounds that Title VII provides the exclusive remedy for discrimination. Lastly, the government argues for the dismissal of the Title VII counts, claming there was no discrimination.

105. *Brown v. Gen. Servs. Admin.*, 45 U.S. 820 (1976).

106. *Id.* at 829, 835.

107. For example, claims pursuant to *Bivens v. Six Unknown Fed. Narcotics Agents*, 403 U.S. 388 (1971).

federal government officials from suit in their individual capacities if at the same time legal action was being taken against the government under Title VII.[108] The court took notice of the concern expressed in *Brown* that it would be easy to avoid administrative procedures and jurisdictional limitations built into Title VII if employment discrimination actions could be brought against the government under other statutory provisions.[109]

Brosnahan found, however, that the ability to sue individual defendants for actions which might constitute federal employment discrimination would not disrupt the statutory scheme of Title VII.[110] The plaintiff, in fact, had fulfilled the procedural requirements of the Civil Rights Act of 1964 and followed the administrative process to its conclusion.[111] The court also noted that the plaintiff sought special remedies, not only equitable relief from employment discrimination.[112] Consequently, the court held that government officials in their individual capacities were not immune from suit for alleged constitutional and statutory violations.[113]

The following year, in *Neely v. Blumenthal*, the question again was raised whether the government's consent to be sued under Title VII extinguished ancillary claims based on *Bivens* theories and directed at federal officials in their individual capacities.[114] In *Neely*, after examining the precise rationale underlying *Brown*, the court concluded that Title VII did not bar related damage claims brought against individuals officers.[115] The court noted that *Brown* did not even address the question of Title VII's preemptive effect on discrimination suits brought against private persons since the plaintiff had not tried to redress his claim of discrimination through legal action against any individual federal official.[116] *Brown* did not settle this point because the issue was never raised.[117]

The court continued on to point out that research disclosed no judicial holding that government consent to being sued extinguished parallel reme-

---

108. *Brosnahan v. Eckerd*, 435 F. Supp. 26 (D.D.C. 1977).

109. *Id.* at 28.

110. *Id.*

111. *Id.*

112. *Id.*

113. *Id.*

114. *Neely v. Blumenthal*, 458 F. Supp. 945, 947 (D.D.C. 1978); *Bivens v. Six Unkown Fed. Narcotics Agents*, 403 U.S. 388 (1971).

115. *Neely*, 458 F. Supp. at 947; *Bivens v. Six Unkown Fed. Narcotics Agents*, 403 U.S. 388 (1971).

116. *Neely*, 458 F. Supp. at 952.

117. *Id.*

dies against individual officers for the same conduct.[118] Using the Federal Tort Claims Act (FTCA) as the model, it noted that the FTCA clearly stated that the waiver of immunity it provided was exclusive.[119] Nonetheless, the exclusivity principle did not contemplate that tort claims under the FTCA precluded action against government employees personally on the grounds that the government had consented to be liable.[120] If it did, the court reasoned,

> there would have been no reason for inserting into the Act a second exclusivity provision that states that, for a certain class of tort injuries… "the remedy against the United States provided" by the Act "shall hereafter be exclusive of any other civil action or proceeding by reason of the same subject matter against the employee…whose act or omission gave rise to the claim."[121]

The court in *Neely*, therefore, concluded that sovereign immunity waivers did not in and of themselves affect pre-existing remedies against individual government officials.[122] Only if the waiver expressed an explicit intent to eliminate other remedies would personal liability be diminished.[123] "[N]othing in Title VII reveals an intent to disturb avenues of relief against discriminating officials in their personal capacities."[124]

Several more recent cases have addressed the question whether Title VII is the exclusive remedy available to federal employees in protected categories who have filed employment discrimination actions and, if not, whether federal officials concurrently or separately can be sued in their individual capacities in torts and for statutory and constitutional violations, as well as for discrimination. In *Wood v. United States*, the court said *Brown* was decided on the basis of sovereign immunity, a doctrine that does not extend to protect government officials from personal liabilities which arise out of their official activities.[125] The court agreed with the reasoning and analysis in *Neely*, also concluding that Congress in passing Title VII and its amendments did not intend to preclude legal action against discriminating individuals in their private capaci-

---

118. *Id.* at 954.
119. *Id.*
120. *Id.*
121. *Id. See also* Federal Tort Claims Act of 1946, 28 U.S.C.A. §§ 2674, 2679(b) (West 1994).
122. *Neely*, 458 F. Supp. at 954.
123. *Id.*
124. *Id.* at 954–55.
125. *Wood v. United States*, 760 F. Supp. 952, 956 (D. Mass. 1991).

ties.[126] *Brown's* preemption rule circumscribed only employment discrimination claims against a federal government agency.[127]

Similarly in *Otto v. Heckler*, the court found that Title VII did not preempt distinct constitutional and tort claims against individual defendants.[128] It decided that the plaintiff's tort claims against her supervisor were not barred, citing as support for its decision Justice Marshall's concurring opinion in *Bush v. Lucas*:

> There is nothing in [this] decision to foreclose a federal employee from pursuing a *Bivens* remedy where his injury is not attributable to personnel actions which may be remedied under the federal statutory scheme."[129]

Other cases have examined whether Title VII provides the exclusive remedy against the government where constitutional or other statutory violations or torts have been alleged for which Title VII provides no protection. In *Ethnic Employees of Library of Congress v. Boorstin*, the court found *Brown's* inquiry involved federal employees bringing parallel actions under both Title VII and other federal laws to redress the same basic injury.[130] It agreed with *Brown* that allowing employees to recast their Title VII claims as constitutional claims would frustrate the legislative policies underlying Title VII.[131] The court in *Ethnic Employees* concluded, however, that Congress did not intend for Title VII to replace those claims for which the Act provided no remedy.[132] Consequently, the *Ethnic Employees'* due process claims and constitutionally protected criticisms of their employer's policies were outside the scope of and not preempted by Title VII.[133]

Jarrell v. Tisch also addressed the question whether under *Brown*, non-Title VII avenues of relief were preempted.[134] The *Jarrell* court's findings agreed with the decision in *Ethnic Employees*. The plaintiff's constitutional claims would be precluded if Title VII remedies sufficiently redressed those claims, but if a

---

126. *Id.*

127. *Id.*

128. *Otto v. Heckler*, 781 F.2d 754, 756-57 (9th Cir. 1986), *amended on other grounds*, 802 F.2d 337 (9th Cir. 1987).

129. *Id.* at 756; *See also Bush v. Lucas*, 462 U.S. 367, 391 (1983).

130. *Ethnic Employees of Library of Congress v. Boorstin*, 751 F.2d 1405, 1415 (D.C. Cir. 1985).

131. *Id.* at 1414.

132. *Id.* at 1415–16.

133. *Id.* at 1415.

134. *Jarrell v. Tisch*, 656 F. Supp. 237, 239 (D.D.C. 1987).

constitutional claim for damages vindicated an interest not protected by Title VII, then *Brown*'s exclusion rule would not apply.[135]

Still other case law indicates that Title VII does not prohibit federal employees who allege employment discrimination from suing for separate causes of action arising out of the same facts. In *Arnold v. United States*, the government again argued that, under *Brown*, Title VII was the exclusive remedy for employment discrimination.[136] The court found the government's analysis incomplete.[137] It determined, instead, that Title VII did not bar remedies for unconstitutional actions other than employment discrimination, even if arising from the same core of facts.[138] The court noted that although the plaintiff had made only vague assertions of constitutional infringements, her allegations of assault, battery, intentional infliction of emotional distress, false imprisonment and harassment were claims sounding in torts.[139] It found her supervisor's alleged behavior beyond the scope of his authority. He had shed his immunity, as a federal government official, by employing illegitimate means and was answerable under state common law tort claims.[140]

In another case, *McAnaw v. Custis*, the defendants, all officials of the Veterans Administrations Medical Center being sued in their official and/or personal capacities for constitutional violations, contended that since the plaintiff had filed an administrative complaint charging sex discrimination based on the same affidavit she filed in court, this suit was merely a gender discrimination action in disguise.[141] The court noted that the plaintiff was making serious First Amendment claims regarding freedom of expression and association. It, therefore, was unwilling to require her to exhaust her administrative remedies for sex discrimination before bringing her *Bivens* action to the district court merely because the two claims arose from related events.[142]

3. Conclusion

In a multi-count complaint which includes claims of unlawful employment discrimination, the government perfunctorily appears to file motions to dis-

---

135. *Id.*

136. *Arnold v. United States*, 816 F.2d 1306, 1311 (9th Cir. 1987).

137. *Id.*

138. *Id.*

139. *Id.* at 1311–12.

140. *Id.* at 1312.

141. *McAnaw v. Custis*, 1982 WL 318, 29 Empl. Prac. Dec. (CCH) at 32,778 (D. Kan. 1982).

142. *Id.*

miss all but Title VII counts from an employee's pleading on the grounds that Title VII provides the exclusive remedy. Where possible then, a plaintiff—alleging violations of the Constitution and/or federal or state laws, as well as discrimination—should draft the complaint to show separate, distinct causes of action. An independent basis should be provided for each claim. Each count should challenge different conduct, assert different interests, implicate rights not protected by Title VII and detail harms not remedied by Title VII. Clearly there is case law indicating that Title VII does not preempt constitutional and statutory violations or state common law torts arising from related or different facts and misconduct, particularly against individual federal agents. Nonetheless, the question of preemption will be a close call for some courts. The more distinct the counts and harms, the better the plaintiff's chances of prevailing in any preclusion argument which the government puts forth.

G. Procedural Matters

Before filing a Title VII complaint against an intelligence agency in district court or with the EEOC, the employee must exhaust all internal administrative procedures. For the CIA employee, for example, the process begins when he or she reports an alleged discriminatory event to the CIA's OEEO. At that time he or she is given a small booklet, "The EEO Process at a Glance."[143] Page 12 provides a chart showing the number of days each phase of the employment discrimination process is supposed to take. The complainant must abide by the timing and deadlines meticulously. No exceptions are made for the employee, and untimeliness is the easiest way for the CIA to dispose of a case. The CIA, on the other hand, may and does delay and obstruct. Although it is supposed to take about one year to exhaust the internal administrative procedures related to an employment discrimination complaint, CIA's tactics have resulted in delaying complainants from filing suit in district court for well over two years, sometimes three.[144] The CIA's administrative processing is neither fast nor easy.

As sympathetic as an officer in the CIA's OEEO may appear, the aggrieved party should be aware that the OEEO is not an independent, impartial body. It is part of the CIA and its employees are paid by and work for the CIA. Its personnel generally consist of other CIA employees on rotational assignments

---

143. *See supra* note 7.
144. *See, e.g., Thompson,* case C, *Conway,* case G.

from their "home" components, to which they will return following their stint in OEEO. Consequently, there is little likelihood that the CIA's OEEO will decide in the employee's favor.

Once the employee receives the CIA OEEO's Final Agency Decision, he or she has 90 days in which to a file a civil action in district court. This means that if the plaintiff's counsel has signed a secrecy agreement with the CIA, the lawyer must submit all documents to the CIA for pre-publication review before filing them in a court of law. The CIA receives advance copies of complaints for redaction well before they are filed in court, a process which opens the door to abuse.

An EEOC hearing is an alternative to district court. The complainant and counsel should be wary of this avenue for the very reason that it is the route preferred by intelligence agencies such as the CIA. First, there is no publicity about a case being heard in the EEOC. Intelligence agencies loathe media coverage of its wrongdoing and misconduct. To prevent the adverse publicity of a case filed in federal court, the government may be more amenable to settle on terms favorable to the plaintiff. Second, the decisions of the EEOC's administrative judges are advisory, and agencies are free to reject or modify them.[145] Federal government employers, including the CIA, however, must comply with holdings of the courts or appeal them.[146] According to an August 17, 1999 "Washington Post" article, the EEOC is particularly weak in enforcing anti-discrimination laws in the federal workplace.[147] Third, intelligence agencies, particularly the CIA, easily and regularly appeal EEOC's decisions, and these appeals may delay the final settlement for years.[148] EEOC critics have

---

145. *See*, Kirstin Grimsley, *EEOC Seeks New Process for Bias Claims Against the U.S.*, Wash. Post, Oct. 3, 1997, at G1, reporting that federal "[g]overnment agencies reverse decisions that are unfavorable to them nearly 63 percent of time, according to EEOC."

146. *See supra* note 1, at §2000e4(g) Powers of Commission (regarding the Power of Commission, the Notes of Decision Index stated that the final responsibility for enforcement was vested with the federal courts).

147. Michael A. Fletcher, *Lubricating the Machinery-EEOC Acts on Criticism That Federal Worker Bias Complaint Process is Clogged*, Wash. Post, Aug. 27, 1999, at A27. This article discussed new regulations to improve the functioning of the EEOC slated to go into effect in November 1999. The tenor of the comments, however, was not optimistic. The pace of EEOC's improvement is contingent on increased funding from Congress for more EEOC judges and attorneys, and Congress thus far is planning no increases in EEOC funding. The article noted that according to the General Accounting Office, even EEOC's efforts to monitor basic job discrimination trends among federal workers was complicated, because EEOC is frequently given faulty data by other agencies.

148. *See Ellis*, case A, originally filed with EEOC in 1987 and continuing more than 10 years.

long complained that government agencies use their power to bog down the federal EEO process.[149]

In a Title VII complaint, the sole defendant is the head of the agency in his official capacity.[150] Individuals may not be sued under Title VII. If a case supports constitutional, non-Title VII statutory or state common law tort claims, however, the plaintiff may be well advised to sue individual federal officials in their personal capacities for their illegal conduct.

Generally the District Court for the Eastern District of Virginia is the federal court where Title VII claims against the CIA are heard. The section of the Civil Rights Act of 1964 which governs venue states:

> an action may be brought in any judicial district in the State in which the unlawful employment practice is alleged to have been committed, in the judicial district in which the employment records relevant to such practice are maintained and administered, or in the judicial district in which the aggrieved person would have worked but for the alleged unlawful employment practice, but if the respondent is not found within any such district, such an action may be brought within the judicial district in which the respondent has his principal office.[151]

Unless the employment discrimination occurred overseas, in one of the CIA's domestic posts, or where the plaintiff would have worked had the discriminatory conduct not occurred, the suit should be filed in Virginia, where CIA headquarters is located, where most of its employees work, where relevant records are or should be maintained, and where the CIA has its principal office. Unfortunately, as noted above, the District Court for the Eastern District of Virginia is conservative and pro-CIA.[152]

H. Damages and Jury Trial

Originally, monetary damages under the Civil Rights Act of 1964 generally were limited to back pay and interest on back pay. In an effort to make the aggrieved party whole again, he or she also was awarded reasonable attorney

---

149. *See supra* note 147.

150. *See supra* note 1, at § 2000e-16(c).

151. *Id.* at § 2000e-5(f)(3).

152. *See* Chapter One, Section A.6.on the special relationship between some Virginia judges and the CIA.

fees.[153] In 1991 Congress amended Title VII to strengthen and improve it and to provide compensatory and punitive damages in cases of intentional employment discrimination.[154] Under the new provisions, a prevailing plaintiff in a Title VII suit against a federal agency, in addition to back pay with interest, could be awarded compensatory damages for future pecuniary losses, emotional pain, suffering, inconvenience, mental anguish, loss of enjoyment of life, and other nonpecuniary losses.[155] The CIA, as a respondent, may be liable for compensatory damages up to $300,000 since it has more than 500 employees.[156] A favorable settlement could mean even more money for the plaintiff.[157] The 1991 Amendment to the Civil Rights Act provides that either party may demand a trial by jury if the complainant is seeking compensatory damages.[158]

---

153. 42 U.S.C.A. § 2000e-5(k) (West 1994).

154. Civil Rights Act of 1991, Pub. L. No. 102-166, 105 Stat. 1071.

155. Civil Rights Act of 1991, Pub. L. No. 102-166, § 102(b)(3), 105 Stat. 1073.

156. *Id.* at § 102(b)(3)(D).

157. *Thompson,* case C, is an example of a settlement in which the plaintiff was awarded over $400,000 in compensatory damages, as well as almost $300,000 in attorney fees and costs.

158. Civil Rights Act of 1991, Pub. L. No. 102-166, § 102(c), 105 Stat. 1073.

CHAPTER FIVE

FEDERAL TORT CLAIMS ACT

With the passage of the Federal Tort Claims Act (FTCA) in 1946, the United States government waived its immunity to suit, but only under certain conditions and in a limited number of circumstances.[1] These conditions and limitations are important in considering whether to embark upon time-consuming and costly litigation against the federal government.

Initially, Chapter Five addresses the co-extensiveness of the federal government's tort liability with a private person's liability in the state in which the suit takes place. Basically, under the FTCA, state tort law determines the United States government's liability. The plaintiff and counsel, therefore, must study the state law governing the commission by a private individual of the particular tort in question to ascertain whether there is a viable cause of action against the federal government.

The discussion then turns to the many exceptions to the FTCA where the United States government would not be liable. Uniquely governmental activities and discretionary acts are excluded even if the acts involve negligence or abuse. Often the court's decision, especially regarding the discretionary act exception, seems to turn on which party's characterization of the conduct is accepted. Libel, slander, misrepresentation and deceit are more clear-cut exceptions. Unless the United States government waives its immunity, it simply cannot be sued for these torts, no matter how much a federal agency or its officials may defame or deceive the plaintiff. In addition and of particular interest to CIA litigants, if the tort occurs abroad, a suit under the FTCA is precluded.

Following the FTCA exceptions analysis, the preclusive effect of a successful tort action is considered. Importantly for the intelligence agency claimant, preclusion does not extend to a civil action against the United States and/or federal agents for unconstitutional conduct or federal statutory violations for which Congress has authorized the action.

---

1. Federal Tort Claims Act (FTCA) of 1946, 28 U.S.C. §2674 *et seq.* and §1346 (West 1994).

The chapter ends with some important procedural requirements and a brief paragraph on damages. State law may govern damages for torts, to include any ceiling on damages.

A. Federal Government's Tort Liability Is Co-Extensive with Private Person's under Applicable State Law

The FTCA gives the district courts:

> exclusive jurisdiction of civil actions on claims against the United States, for money damages…for injury or loss of property, or personal injury or death caused by the negligent or wrongful act or omission of any employee of the government while acting within the scope of his office or *employment, under circumstances where the United States, if a private person, would be liable to the claimant in accordance with the law of the place where the act or omission occurred* (emphasis added).[2]

The Act adds that:

> The United States shall be liable…*in the same manner and to the same extent as a private individual under like circumstances,* but shall not be liable for interest prior to judgment or for punitive damages. (emphasis added).[3]

Courts have interpreted "in the same manner and to the same extent as a private individual under like circumstances" to mean that state tort law determines the federal government's liability.

In *Proud v. United States*, for example, a young girl sustained injuries in a diving accident at a National Park in Hawaii.[4] The applicable Hawaiian statute stated that a landowner owed no duty of care to keep his premises safe for entry or use by others for recreational purposes or to give any warning of dangerous conditions. The court decided that since the FTCA provided that the federal government's tort liability was co-extensive with that of a private per-

---

2. *Id.* at § 1346.
3. *Id.* at § 2674.
4. *Proud v. United States*, 723 F.2d 705 (9th Cir. 1984).

son under the law of the state and a private landowner would not be liable for the child's injuries, neither was the United States.[5]

This co-extensive with state law principle means, for example, that if a CIA litigant filed an FTCA claim in the District Court for the Eastern District of Virginia, Virginia state law would be applicable. If a private person were liable for a particular type of tort in Virginia, the government similarly would be liable, as long as the conduct or negligence did not fall under one of the exceptions. Conversely, as in *Proud*, there would be no government liability where an individual defendant would not be held liable. Also, since the FTCA makes the federal government's liability turn on that of a private individual under like circumstances, if Virginia law capped tort damages at a certain sum, the United States' financial liability to the CIA employee similarly would be limited.

B. Exceptions

1. Uniquely Governmental Activities

When considering a suit under the FTCA, it is important to look at the many exceptions. In addition to interpreting the phrase "in the same manner and to the same extent as a private individual under like circumstances" to mean that the United States government's tort liability is co-extensive with a private individual's under applicable state law, the Supreme Court has construed it to mean that the government has no liability for the performance of uniquely governmental functions, even if conducted negligently.[6]

In *Feres v. United States*, for example, the Supreme Court said that it did not believe Congress created a new cause of action dependent on local law for military service-connected injuries and deaths due to negligence.[7] Consequently, the Court held that the federal government was not liable under the FTCA for service-related injuries or deaths arising out of an activity incident to military service.[8] The rationale for this was that the relationship between the government and members of the armed forces was "distinctively federal in character...."[9]

---

5. *Id.* at 707.
6. *Indian Towing Co. v. United States*, 350 U.S. 61, 64 (1955).
7. *Feres v. United States*, 340 U.S. 135, 146 (1950).
8. *Id.*
9. *Id.* at 143.

In the seminal case, *Indian Towing Co. v. United States*, on the other hand, a divided Supreme Court noted that "all government activity is inescapably 'uniquely governmental' in that it is performed by the government."[10] This exception for uniquely governmental functions, therefore, could negate any claim under the FTCA, making the Act virtually nebulous. Realizing that re-enforcing the federal government's immunity to suit was not the Congressional intent underlying the FTCA, the Court held that liability could be found pursuant to the FTCA against the Coast Guard for the negligent operation of a lighthouse light. In this case, the Court interpreted the statutory language "under like circumstances" to mean that, under tort law, one who undertakes to warn the public of danger and, thereby, induces reliance has a duty to use due care.[11] The Coast Guard had an obligation to ensure the lighthouse was kept in good working order, to use due care to discover failure of a light, and to repair it or give warning it was not functioning.[12]

Two years later, in *Rayonier Inc. v. United States*, the Supreme Court affirmed its *Indian Towing Co.* decision.[13] In a suit involving the United States' liability for the negligence of its Forest Service employees in fighting fires, the government argued that neither the common law nor the law in the state where the fire occurred imposed liability on municipal or local governments for the negligence of their agents acting in the "uniquely governmental" capacity of firemen.[14] The Court disagreed. It noted that it had expressly decided that "an injured party cannot be deprived of his rights under the Act by resort to an alleged distinction... between the Government's negligence when it acts in a 'proprietary' capacity and its negligence when it acts in a 'uniquely governmental' capacity."[15] It added that the very purpose of the FTCA was to waive the government's traditional all-encompassing immunity from torts and to establish "novel and unprecedented" government liability.[16] The Court found no justification to read exemptions into the FTCA beyond those provided by Congress. It pointed out that if the Act were to be amended, the body which adopted the FTCA would have that function.[17]

In the 1984 *United States v. Varig Airlines* case, the Supreme Court chose the road of judicial avoidance when confronted with this concept of a

---

10. *See supra* note 6, at 67.
11. *Id.* at 64–65.
12. *Id.* at 67.
13. *Rayonier Inc. v. United States*, 352 U.S. 315 (1957).
14. *Id.* at 318–19.
15. *Id.* at 319.
16. *Id.*
17. *Id.* at 320.

"uniquely governmental" activity.[18] Here the issue presented was whether the Federal Aviation Administration (FAA) could be held liable under the FTCA for its negligence in certifying certain aircraft for use in commercial aviation. The government asserted that the conduct of the FAA in certifying aircraft was a core governmental activity which was not actionable under the FTCA because no private individual engaged in analogous activity.[19] The Court decided to rest its decision on the discretionary functions exception to the FTCA, and, therefore, found it unnecessary to address the "uniquely governmental" activity issue.[20]

Since the federal government has not prevailed in the Supreme Court on the matter of a "uniquely governmental" activity under the FTCA, if it asserts this argument at all, the United States probably will hedge its bets by claiming other exceptions to the FTCA along with it. The most likely argument in the alternative would be the exception for discretionary functions.

2. Discretionary Functions

Under the FTCA, all discretionary acts are excluded, even if the discretion involves abuse. Section 2680(a) specifies that the FTCA does not apply to:

> Any claim based upon an act or omission of an employee of the government, exercising due care, in the execution of a statute or regulation, whether or not such a statute or regulation be valid, or based upon the exercise or performance or *the failure to exercise or perform a discretionary function or duty on the part of a federal agency or an employee of the government, whether or not the discretion involved be abused* (emphasis added).[21]

This discretionary function exception to the FTCA appears to be the most difficult and contentious part of section 2680. As with the interpretation of "uniquely governmental" functions, if construed too broadly, this exception could "completely swallow the waiver of immunity."[22]

In order to defeat the discretionary function exception, a two-tier analysis is necessary. First, the plaintiff must show there was no room for judgment, decision or discretion in the government's action taken against him or her. For

---

18. *United States v. Varig Airlines*, 467 U.S. 797, 814 (1984).
19. *Id.* at n.12.
20. *Id.*
21. *See supra* note 1, at § 2680(a).
22. *Dalehite v. United States*, 346 U.S. 15, 57 (1953) (warning given by Justice Jackson).

example, an FTCA claim would not be barred if specific regulations prohibited the conduct. Second, the claimant must establish that no considerations of governmental or public policy were involved.

How broadly the discretionary function exception has been defined by the Supreme Court is demonstrated in the test case, *Dalehite v. United States*.[23] Here, fertilizer with an ammonium nitrate base stored in a vessel in Texas harbor exploded and caused death, injury and property damage, resulting in 300 claims for the aggregate amount of two hundred million dollars. The plaintiffs alleged negligence on the part of the concerned federal officials and employees in the production of the fertilizer.[24]

The Supreme Court noted that the history of the FTCA indicated Congress did not contemplate that the government should be held liable for a claim arising from an act of a governmental nature or function or for results of an act of discretion in the performance of a governmental function,[25] even though the act was negligently performed and/or involved the abuse of discretion.[26] What was protected, according to the Court, was the discretion of executives and administrators to act in accordance with their own judgment as to the best course.[27] This protection included determinations made by executives and administrators in establishing plans, specifications or schedules of operations[28] and in the propriety of discretionary administrative acts.[29] Where there was room for policy judgment and decision, discretion existed.[30] From this decision, the Court reasoned that acts of subordinates in carrying out operations of the government in accordance with official directions could not be actionable.[31] It said that the FTCA required some kind of misfeasance or nonfeasance, and, therefore, did not extend to liability without fault.[32] The majority concluded that the conduct of the government in formulating a plan for manufacturing fertilizer and in implementing the plan were acts of discretion, carrying no liability. Judgment was rendered for the United States.

Over thirty years later, in the case of *Berkovitz v. United States*, the Supreme Court further clarified the discretionary function and provided a good exam-

---

23. *Id.*
24. *Id.* at 17, 18.
25. *Id.* at 28.
26. *Id.* at 30.
27. *Id.* at 34.
28. *Id.* at 35–36.
29. *Id.* at 27.
30. *Id.* at 36.
31. *Id.*
32. *Id.* at 45.

ple where the exception was not applicable under the FTCA.[33] In this suit, a two-month old infant contracted polio from an oral polio vaccine that did not comply with regulatory standards. The Court held that the National Institute of Health's Division of Biologic Standards (DBS) had no discretion to issue a license to a laboratory to produce a certain oral polio vaccine without first receiving the required test data. To do so violated a specific statutory and regulatory directive.[34] Also, the Court noted that if the DBS issued a license either without determining whether the vaccine complied with regulatory standards or after determining the vaccine failed to comply, the discretionary function did not bar the claim.[35] Further, if DBS' policy did not allow officials to release a noncomplying lot of polio vaccine, the discretionary function exception did not bar the claim. The Court concluded that should the plaintiff be able to demonstrate that the government's conduct did not involve the permissible exercise of policy discretion, the government's invocation of the discretionary function exception would be improper.[36]

In *Berkovitz*, the Supreme Court discussed policy judgments. It explained that the basis of the discretionary function exception was Congress' desire to "prevent judicial 'second-guessing' of legislative and administrative decisions grounded in social, economic, and political policy through the medium of an action in tort."[37] The exception, therefore, protected only governmental actions and decisions based on considerations of public policy. The discretionary function exception insulated the government from liability if the challenged action involved the permissible exercise of policy judgment.[38] The Court continued on, however, to reject the government's contention that the exception precluded liability for any and all acts arising out of regulatory programs of federal agencies.[39]

The Supreme Court's decision in *United States v. Gaubert* similarly combined the requirements for a judgment or choice based on considerations of public policy.[40] In this case, however, the Court made the sweeping and somewhat surprising generalization that "[w]hen established governmental policy, as expressed or implied by statute, regulation, or agency guidelines, allows a

---

33. *Berkovitz v. United States*, 486 U.S. 531 (1988).
34. *Id.* at 542–43.
35. *Id.* at 544.
36. *Id.* at 547–48.
37. *Id.* at 536–37; *see also United States v. Varig Airlines*, 467 U.S. 797, 814 (1984).
38. *Berkovitz*, 486 U.S. at 537.
39. *Id.* at 538.
40. *United States v. Gaubert*, 499 U.S. 315 (1991).

government agent to exercise discretion, it must be presumed that the agent's acts are grounded in policy when exercising that discretion."[41]

Gaubert, the chairman of the board and the largest shareholder in a Texas-chartered and federally-insured savings and loan association, brought action against the United States under the FTCA, alleging negligent supervision by the directors and officers and negligent involvement in day-to-day operations by the Federal Home Loan Bank regulators. Gaubert sought damages for the lost value of his shares and for the property he forfeited under his personal guarantee of the bank's worth.

The Court decided that each of the challenged actions—planning-level decisions, promulgation of regulations to carry out programs and actions taken in furtherance of programs—even if negligent, contained a large element of judgment or choice and were, therefore, protected.[42] Further, each regulatory action was based on public policy considerations involving the kind of policy judgment which the discretionary function exception was designed to shield.[43] Since the actions of the federal regulators involved: (1) the exercise of discretion and (2) were taken in furtherance of public policy goals, Gaubert's claims were barred by the discretionary function exception.[44]

Although case precedent provides some guidelines on how to interpret discretionary acts, a court's decision often seems to be based on its acceptance of a party's characterization of the conduct. Consequently, in characterizing an FTCA claim against the CIA, for instance for negligent hiring, negligent supervision or infliction of emotional distress, the litigant should explain in a concrete manner the specific action(s) on which the claim is based and show there is a governmental or CIA regulation or policy against such conduct. Then the complainant needs to demonstrate that no government policy considerations are involved.

In the case of *Jill*, case J, for example, there was some evidence that before joining the CIA, the Agency officer who assaulted and attempted to rape Jill might have committed a similar act upon another female. Given the CIA's extensive and thorough pre-hiring investigation and stringent hiring policy, this officer's earlier history, if indeed he had assaulted and/or attempted to rape another woman, should have been uncovered and he should not have been hired by the CIA. There should be no room for discretion or judgment as to

---

41. *Id.* at 324.
42. *Id.* at 323.
43. *Id.* at 332.
44. *Id.* at 334.

whether to hire such an individual. Hence had Jill's case not been settled, Jill might have had a solid case against the government under the FTCA for negligent hiring. The CIA, on the other hand, might try to characterize its hiring policy as a discretionary function, which even if performed negligently, would be barred as an FTCA claim.[45] Jill, however, should have been able to establish the existence of a CIA policy not only against the alleged perpetrator's conduct, but also against hiring someone who has committed such a crime. In addition, no government or public policy considerations would be involved here. To the contrary, government policy is to take a strong stance against such behavior.

3. Libel, Slander, Misrepresentation, and Deceit

Other FTCA exceptions preclude a lawsuit against the federal government for libel, slander, misrepresentation and deceit. Specifically under section 2680(h), the FTCA excludes:

[A]ny claim arising out of assault, battery, false imprisonment, false arrest, malicious prosecution, abuse of process, libel, slander, misrepresentation, deceit, or interference with contract rights.[46]

Governmental immunity for libel and slander is particularly important for a CIA litigant because retaliation, which takes the form of defamation and ruination of an employee's good name and reputation, is commonplace when an aggrieved party files a legal action against the CIA. Courts have confirmed, however, that the FTCA bars claims arising out of libel or slander.[47]

---

45. The government also could also argue that: (a) provision 2680(h) of the FTCA makes an exception for any claim against the government arising out of assault and battery; (b) the CIA officer was off-duty when the assault and attempted rape occurred; (c) the assault was intentional; and/or (d) the assault took place overseas. In *Sheridan v. United States*, 487 U.S. 392 (1988), the Supreme Court held that in at least some situations the fact that the injury was directly caused by an assault and battery would not preclude liability against the government for negligently allowing the assault to occur. Also, the Court noted that the assailant's off-duty status did not protect the government, nor did characterizing his behavior as intentional.

46. *See supra* note 1, at § 2680(h).

47. *See, e.g., Aviles v. Lutz*, 887 F.2d 1046, 1049 (10th Cir. 1989).

Similarly, negligent as well as deliberate misrepresentation and deceit are not actionable under the FTCA.[48] If, however, the damage arose out of a legal duty to use due care by providing accurate and adequate information, then the claim could be actionable.[49]

The courts construe the misrepresentation exception broadly when damages result from the plaintiff's reliance upon false or inadequate information provided by the government.[50] These misrepresentation and deceit exceptions are highly significant to employees litigating against the CIA since, unfortunately, plaintiffs could rely to their detriment on false information purposely provided by the Agency. The CIA is skilled in such conduct and has used it against employees who decide to fight back. This problem is exacerbated by the CIA's control of most, if not all, of the information required by the litigant. Under the FTCA, however, the federal government could not be sued for the CIA's misrepresentation and deception in providing false or misleading information to employees or their counsel.

4. Foreign Country

Of particular interest to those CIA employees who spend much of their careers serving abroad may be the FTCA exception of any claim arising in a foreign country. If the injury occurs overseas, the suit is precluded. Section 2680(k) specifically states the FTCA does not apply to "[a]ny claim arising in a foreign country."[51]

In *United States v. Smith*, the Smiths filed a lawsuit alleging a military doctor had negligently injured their baby during its birth at a United States Army hospital in Italy.[52] The lower court dismissed the case, holding that the FTCA precluded recovery for injuries obtained abroad.[53] On appeal, the Supreme Court confirmed this decision and further barred legal action against the doctor personally, foreclosing the possibility of pursuing an alternative mode of recovery for a tort claim against the government employee who allegedly caused the injury.[54]

---

48. *United States v. Neustadt*, 366 U.S. 696, 702 (1961).
49. As it was in *Indian Towing Co.*, *see supra* note 6.
50. *Frigard v. United States*, 862 F.2d 201, 202 (9th Cir. 1988).
51. *See supra* note 1, at §2680(k).
52. *United States v. Smith*, 499 U.S. 160 (1991).
53. *Id.*
54. *Id.* at 162.

C. Preclusion

The FTCA, section 2679, states that:

The authority of any federal agency to sue and be sued in its own name shall not be construed to authorize suits against such federal agency on claims which are cognizable under...this title, and the *remedies provided by title shall be exclusive.* (emphasis added)[55]

Emphasizing the exclusiveness of this remedy, section 2679(b)(1) adds:

The remedy against the United States provided [in this title]...*for injury or loss of property, or personal injury or death arising or resulting from the negligent or wrongful act or omission of any employee of the government while acting within the scope of his office or employment is exclusive of any other civil action or proceeding for money damages by reason of the same subject matter against the employee whose act or omission gave rise to the claim or against the estate of such employee. Any other civil action or proceeding for money damages arising out of or relating to the same subject matter against the employee or the employee's estate is precluded without regard to when the act or omission occurred.* (emphasis added)[56]

Nonetheless, and very important for the intelligence agency employee-litigant, is the fact that this preclusion:

does not extend or apply to a civil action against an employee of the government—
(A) which is brought for a violation of the Constitution of the United States, or
(B) which is brought for a violation of a statute of the United States under which such action an individual is otherwise authorized.[57]

Circumstances permitting, therefore, intelligence agency employees concurrently with or separately from an FTCA action against the United States government could bring a *Bivens*-type suit against individual intelligence officers who, while acting under the color of law, allegedly violated their constitutional

---

55. *See supra* note 1, at § 2679(a).
56. *Id.* at § 2679(b)(1).
57. *Id.* at § 2679(b)(2).

rights.[58] Conceivably, also, an employment discrimination action, specifically authorized under Title VII, could be pursued along with an FTCA claim.

D. Procedural Matters

The statute of limitations in a tort action against the federal government is two years. Section 2401(b) of Title 28 states:

> A tort claim against the United States shall be forever barred unless it is presented in writing to the appropriate federal agency within two years after such a claim accrues or unless action is begun within six months after the date of mailing...of notice of final denial of the claim by the agency to which it was presented.[59]

If the time lapses before a suit is filed, counsel may try to argue the doctrine of equitable estoppel, especially if the intelligence agency obfuscated the problem and concealed material facts that could have served as the basis for bringing an earlier action. Since the federal government exploits the timeliness issue to move for the dismissal of claims,[60] however, it is advisable to carefully observe deadlines.

Before filing an FTCA claim in federal district court, a complainant against an intelligence agency must first present his or her claim with his or her agency and exhaust all internal administrative remedies.[61] This action is initiated by submitting a standard form, the SF 95.[62]

FTCA, section 2675, states:

> An action shall not be instituted...unless the claimant shall have first presented the claim to the appropriate federal agency and his claim shall have been finally denied by the agency in writing and sent by certified or registered mail. The failure of any agency to make final disposition of a claim within six months after it is filed shall, at the

---

58. *Bivens*, 403 U.S. at 390.
59. 28 U.S.C.A. § 2401(b) (West 1994).
60. *Thompson*, case C; *see Thompson v. Woolsey*, Motion to Partially Dismiss, Civ. Action No. 94-923A (E.D. Va. Sept. 23, 1994), where the government tried to have the tort claims dismissed on the grounds that they were untimely.
61. 28 U.S.C.A. § 2675 (West 1994).
62. 28 C.F.R. § 14.2(a) (1999).

option of the claimant any time thereafter, be deemed a final denial of the claim.... [63]

Gould v. United States Department of Health & Human Services. confirmed that disposition by a federal agency is a prerequisite to filing an FTCA law suit. [64]

The claim under the FTCA must state a sum certain in money damages. Failure to specify a sum could result in the dismissal of the suit. [65]

It appears also that an individual defendant employee may be sued in his or her personal capacity for a common law tort violation unless the United States Attorney General or the Department of Justice, Director of the Torts Branch, certifies that the defendant employee was acting within the scope of his or her federal employment when the incident out of which the claim arose occurred. If and when this certification is made, a suit sounding in torts against an individual federal agent is replaced by an action against the United States as the party defendant. A proceeding under the FTCA against the federal government may not go forward without this certification. [66]

In *Johnson v. Carter,* the court affirmed that when the director of the Department of Justice's tort claims branch certifies that an individual acted within the scope of his employment during the events underlying the plaintiff's suit, the federal government then must be substituted for the individual being sued. [67] The court in *Aviles v. Lutz* made a similar determination, noting that an FTCA action must be brought against the United States, not against a specific government agency. [68] With the official certification that the defendant was acting within the scope of his or her employment, the individual CIA employee(s) who was allegedly responsible for the tort, as well as the CIA itself, becomes immune to an action under the FTCA.

---

63. 28 U.S.C. §2675 (West 1994).

64. *Gould v. United States Dep't of Health & Human Servs.,* 905 F.2d. 738, 741 (4th Cir. 1990), *cert. denied,* 498 U.S. 1025 (1991).

65. *College v. United States,* 572 F.2d 453, 454 (4th Cir. 1978).

66. *Westfall v. Erwin,* 484 U.S. 292 (1988), commonly known as the Westfall Act. The Westfall Act amended the FTCA to remove potential personal liability of federal government employees for torts committed within the scope of their employment. The exclusive tort remedy, instead, is an action against the United States under the FTCA. Federal Employees Liability Reform and Tort Compensation Act of 1988, Pub. L. No. 100-694, 102 Stat 4563; *See also supra* note 1, at §2679.

67. *Johnson v. Carter,* 983 F.2d. 1316, 1319-20 (4th Cir. 1993), *cert. denied,* 510 U.S. 812, 114 S. Ct. 57 (1993).

68. *See supra* note 47, at 1048.

E. Damages

The FTCA imposes no ceiling on judgments or settlements. Congress provides continuing appropriations for payments over $2,500. Any amount under $2,500 is paid by the head of the concerned federal agency out of the appropriations available to that agency.[69] Nonetheless, the state law in the state where the claim is litigated may provide a cap on damages in a suit sounding in torts.

The complainant should be aware that section 2672 of the FTCA specifies that the acceptance of an "award, compromise, or settlement is final and conclusive on claimant, and shall constitute a complete release of any claim against the United States and against the employee of the government whose act or omission gave rise to the claim, by reason of same subject matter."[70] Once an FTCA claim is decided by the courts or in settlement, it is final. Neither the government nor any individual government employee remains liable. Unless the plaintiff has claims against individual government employees for constitutional violations or against a government agency or its employee(s) for violations of a federal statute which authorizes such civil actions, the plaintiff may not continue to sue the government or any government employee for the same conduct or negligence and will be awarded no further damages.

Also, attorney fees are regulated under the FTCA. Section 2678 specifies that legal fees may not exceed twenty-five percent of any judgment or twenty percent of any award, compromise, or settlement.[71]

F. Conclusion

Pitfalls, indeed, exist for an intelligence agency employee filing an FTCA action. To prevent a time-consuming and costly lawsuit, only to have the court determine that litigation under the FTCA is foreclosed, close attention must be paid to situations where the FTCA would not be applicable. These exceptions include uniquely governmental or discretionary acts, claims of libel, slander, misrepresentation or deceit and claims arising in a foreign country. The conditions and limitations where an individual is not permitted to sue may lead to a decision against filing a tort action under the FTCA.

---

69. *See supra* note 1, at § 2672.
70. *See supra* note 1, at § 2672.
71. *Id.* at § 2678.

Counsel and the injured employee also must carefully weigh the benefits of a successful tort action against any preclusive effect it could have on related litigation. Preclusion does not extend to a civil action against an individual government employee brought for violations of the Constitution or federal laws under which such action is otherwise authorized. Consequently, a *Bivens* action against an individual CIA official for the denial of an employee's constitutional rights and a Title VII suit naming the Director of the CIA as the party defendant in an employment discrimination case may be pursued concurrently with a tort claim against the federal government pursuant to the FTCA. The plaintiff may have much to gain and little to lose by filing an FTCA action together with or separate from these other claims. If he or she prevails, the FTCA provides no damage cap, although state law may.

Employees who decide to file FTCA actions must carefully observe every procedural requirement. The government is unforgiving concerning regulations such as statutes of limitation and stating a sum certain in money damages. The United States can choose not to follow the rules; the litigant cannot.

CHAPTER SIX

CONSTITUTIONAL VIOLATIONS, *BIVENS* AND ITS PROGENY

In 1971, the Supreme Court made an important decision which has had far-reaching consequences. It held federal government officers responsible for their illegal conduct. In *Bivens v. Six Unknown Federal Narcotics Agents*, the Court found that when federal agents acting under color of law violated a person's Fourth amendment rights, the victim was entitled to recover money damages.[1] In later cases, the Supreme Court extended its decision to cover other unconstitutional acts for which individual federal officials could be held personally liable. The holdings, at least in the lower courts, indicate that even where there are available statutory and tort remedies, a suit against individual federal employees for violating a person's constitutional rights would not be precluded.

Applying these *Bivens*-type decisions to a plaintiff taking legal action against an intelligence agency, it appears that an intelligence agency employee could sue individual intelligence officials for violating his or her constitutional rights. Intelligence agency employees likely are entitled under *Bivens* to a due process liberty interest, as well as a right to procedural due process. CIA officers have no guarantee to continued employment, but they may have a property interest in career growth and professional status and, albeit limited due to the secrecy agreement an employee must sign, a First Amendment right to freedom of expression and to petition their elected officials and, of course, the courts for redress of grievances.

In a case against an intelligence agency, the defendants generally argue for qualified immunity, claiming they were performing a discretionary function and the right was not clearly established. To defeat the government's case for immunity, counsel for the plaintiff should be prepared to argue that the defendants knew or reasonably should have known that their conduct violated the plaintiff's constitutional rights.

---

1. *Bivens*, 403 U.S. at 390.

A. *Bivens* Remedy for Violation of Constitutional Rights by Federal Agent

In *Bivens v. Six Unknown Federal Narcotics Agents*, Webster Bivens claimed to have suffered great humiliation, embarrassment and mental suffering when federal narcotics agents unlawfully and unreasonably searched and arrested him in violation of the Fourth Amendment to the Constitution. Justice Brennan, speaking for the Court, pointed out that a federal agent acting unconstitutionally in the name of the United States "possesses a far greater capacity for harm than an individual…exercising no authority other than his own."[2] He noted that the Fourth Amendment's prohibition against unreasonable searches and seizures served as a limitation upon that exercise of federal power.[3] Consequently, when a federal agent acting under color of his authority violates this Amendment, such conduct gives rise to a cause of action for damages.[4]

The Court then addressed the specific question of damages, acknowledging that while the Fourth Amendment did not in so many words provide for enforcement by awarding money, "it is…well settled that where legal rights have been invaded…federal courts may use any available remedy to make good the wrong done."[5] The Court, therefore, held that Bivens was entitled to recover money damages for injuries he suffered as a result of the federal agents' unconstitutional conduct.[6]

B. Extension of *Bivens* to Other Constitutional Violations

Bivens focused on a claim against federal officials acting under color of law who violated a person's Fourth Amendment rights. Since that ruling, the Supreme Court has extended *Bivens* to include several other unconstitutional actions taken by United States government officers who were acting in their official capacities. The Court also addressed the question of whether or not these officials were immune from suit.

---

2. *Id.* at 392.
3. *Id.* at 394.
4. *Id.* at 389.
5. *Id.* at 396.
6. *Id.* at 397.

In *Butz v. Economou*, for example, Economou alleged several unconstitutional actions by Department of Agriculture officials in retaliation for his critical comments about its staff and operations.[7] The plaintiff charged that federal officers had wrongfully initiated administrative proceedings against him without proper notice, had furnished administrative complaints to interested persons without the plaintiff's answers, and had issued a press release containing facts which the defendants knew or should have known were false. These actions, he claimed, denied him his constitutional rights to due process of law and privacy. Additionally, he alleged that the defendants discouraged and chilled his criticism of them, thereby depriving him of his right of free expression as guaranteed by the First Amendment.[8] The Supreme Court in *Butz* did not decide these constitutional issues but answered questions on immunity and remanded the *Bivens* claims to the lower court with instructions.[9]

The following year the Supreme Court, in *Davis v. Passman*, recognized that Fifth Amendment violations were cognizable under *Bivens*.[10] In this case, a former Congressional staffer, who was fired because the Congressman for whom she worked wanted a man as his understudy, sued the legislator for sexual discrimination in violation of the due process clause of the Fifth Amendment.[11]

Speaking for the Court, Justice Brennan quoted the Fifth Amendment prohibition against the deprivation "of life, liberty or property, without due process of law." He provided examples of the numerous decisions in which the Supreme Court had held that the due process clause of the Fifth Amendment forbade the federal government from denying equal protection under the law.[12] He concluded that the Fifth Amendment indeed conferred upon the plaintiff the constitutional right to be free from illegal discrimination, especially since she was in a category of employees (Congressional staffers) unprotected by Title VII.[13]

Justice Brennan then discussed the concept of a "cause of action." He acknowledged that statutory rights and obligations were established by Congress, which determined who may enforce these rights and in what manner.[14] With

---

7. *Butz v. Economou*, 438 U.S. 478 (1978).

8. *Id.* at 483.

9. *See* Chapter Two—Sovereign Immunity, Section B for the Court's decisions on immunity.

10. *Davis v. Passman*, 442 U.S. 228 (1979).

11. *Id.* at 230 n.3.

12. *Id.* at 234.

13. *Id.* at 236.

14. *Id.* at 241.

constitutionally designated rights, on the other hand, he said, "the judiciary is clearly discernible as the primary means through which these rights may be enforced."[15] Indeed, he noted, the Supreme Court had already settled that a cause of action may be implied directly under the equal protection component of the Fifth Amendment's due process clause in favor of the party seeking to enforce this right.[16] Moreover, the Court decided that, as in *Bivens*, the plaintiff's injury may be redressed by a money damage remedy.[17]

Carlson v. Green further extended *Bivens* to cover Eighth Amendment proscriptions against cruel and unusual punishment.[18] In this case, a mother brought suit on behalf of her son who died from personal injuries because federal prison officials failed to give him proper medical care. The Supreme Court concluded that the survival of Green's *Bivens* cause of action was determined by federal common law, rather than relevant state survival statutes. It reasoned that the liability of federal agents for unconstitutional conduct should not turn on the location where the violation occurred.[19]

In *Bishop v. Tice*, the Eighth Circuit court distinguished substantive and procedural due process rights under the Fifth Amendment.[20] In this case, Bishop, a career-status safety engineer, claimed that three federal employees of the Occupational Safety and Health Administration threatened that if he did not resign within one hour, they would lodge criminal charges against him. They refused to state the nature or the details of the charges or to allow him to consult an attorney or leave the room. Bishop, therefore, was forced to resign from his position without availing himself of any civil service administrative remedies.[21]

In his suit, Bishop characterized his substantive due process rights as both a property interest in continued federal employment, absent a showing of good cause for his dismissal, and a liberty interest in his standing and reputation in the community.[22] The court dismissed his substantive claims because of the existence of civil service remedies.[23] Since the defendants allegedly blocked his resort to administrative remedies, however, the court held Bishop

---

15. *Id.*
16. *Id.* at 242.
17. *Id.* at 247–48.
18. *Carlson v. Green*, 446 U.S. 14 (1980).
19. *Id.* at 24.
20. *Bishop v. Tice*, 622 F.2d 349 (8th Cir. 1980).
21. *Id.* at 352.
22. *Id.* at 354.
23. *Id.* at 357.

could proceed against these federal officials for interference with his right to procedural due process.[24] It added that if Bishop proved his case, he would be entitled to the damages that actually occurred, including mental and emotional distress.[25]

In yet another case, *Grichenko v. United States Postal Service*, the plaintiff alleged that federal officials intentionally failed to process in a timely manner his application for compensation under the Federal Employees' Compensation Act (FECA).[26] When he finally filed a notice of claim after learning postal service employees had not done so, his claim was denied on the basis that he had not made a timely application.[27] The district court agreed that the failure of federal officials to timely process his claim deprived the plaintiff of the opportunity to use the administrative remedies provided under FECA to present a disability application to the Department of Labor and violated his Fifth Amendment constitutional rights by denying him procedural due process. Grichenko, therefore, had a separate *Bivens*-type cause of action for deprivation of his constitutional rights in addition to whatever other claims he had under FECA.[28]

C. *Bivens*, As Applied to U.S. Intelligence

The Fifth Amendment's prohibition against the deprivation "of life, liberty or property, without due process of law," the right to equal protection of the laws, and the First Amendment guarantees of freedom to assemble and petition the government for redress of grievances provide the people of the United States with a variety of constitutional rights and privileges. These include substantive due process property and liberty guarantees, as well as related procedural due process rights. Intelligence agency employees, including those working for the CIA, enjoy at least some of these rights.

1. Property Interest

Property interests…are not created by the Constitution. Rather, they are created and their dimensions are defined by existing rules or un-

---

24. *Id.*
25. *Id.*
26. *Grichenko v. United States Postal Serv.*, 524 F. Supp. 672, 673 (E.D.N.Y. 1981).
27. *Id.* at 674.
28. *Id.* at 677–78.

derstandings that stem from an independent source such as state law (or statutes)—rules or understandings that secure certain benefits and that support claims of entitlement to those benefits.[29]

Intelligence agencies have rules, policies, and regulations that secure certain benefits—certain property interests—for its employees. These rules and understandings support claims of entitlement to equitable and unbiased treatment of its personnel and their grievances. Intelligence officials also are required to abide by federal statutes and the Constitution of the United States.

"In performance-based actions, an employee is entitled to certain substantive due process rights."[30] Generally, property interests encompass the right to continued federal employment absent a showing of good cause for dismissal, to a livelihood and career progression, and to merited assignments and promotions without prejudice or interference by federal officials in violation of a government agency's policies, procedures and regulations.[31]

As discussed, however, in Chapter Three, Section C, of the Administrative Procedure Act (APA), the Supreme Court in *Webster v. Doe* found that termination decisions taken by the Director of the CIA under the National Security Act (NSA), section 102(c) authorizing termination, when necessary or advisable, in the interests of the United States, were not judicially reviewable under the APA.[32] Nonetheless, the Court recognized that nothing in the NSA demonstrated that Congress meant to preclude consideration of colorable constitutional claims arising out of the Director's action.[33]

Consequently, the plaintiff in *Webster v. Doe* brought a *Bivens* claim for violating his Fifth Amendment due process property interests, this time in the suit *Doe v. Gates*.[34] The Court of Appeals, District of Columbia Circuit, however, decided against Doe. It found that the law was clear: "[I]f a statute relegates termination decisions to the discretion of the Director, no property en-

29. This standard was established in the *Bd. of Regents v. Roth*, 408 U.S. 564, 577 (1978) and followed in *Cleveland Bd. of Educ. v. Loudermill*, 470 U.S. 532, 538 (1985).

30. *Bowden v. Dep't of Army*, 59 M.S.P.R. 662 (1993).

31. In *LaChance v. Erickson*, 522 U.S. 262, 266 (1998), the Supreme Court noted that the Fifth Amendment provides no person shall be deprived of his or her property without due process of law. The Court then said that it assumed to be correct the Court of Appeals statement, "it is undisputed that…government employees…had a property interest in their employment."

32. *Webster v. Doe*, 486 U.S. 592 (1988).

33. *Id.* at 593.

34. *Doe v. Gates*, 981 F.2d 1316 (D.C. Cir. 1993).

titlement exists."[35] This decision was affirmed in *Dickson v. United States*, when the court determined that despite Dickson's professional status, training experience, and seniority of 20 years with the CIA, he had no protectible property interest in continued employment.[36]

The question still remains, however, whether CIA employees have constitutionally cognizable property interests if they continue to work for the CIA but find their career growth and merited assignments and promotions blocked by CIA officials who are violating the CIA's own policies and regulations. The property interest of an intelligence agency officer in his or her own professional status and career growth, unlike termination, may be subject to judicial review.

2. Liberty Interest

Due process liberty interests are among the Fifth Amendment rights all Americans possess, and the termination of an intelligence agency officer's employment may be judicially reviewable under a liberty interest rubric in certain circumstances. A liberty interest is implicated where a government agency negatively alters the employment status of its employee and in doing so stigmatizes the employee or impugns his or her reputation so as to either (1) seriously damage his or her standing and associations in the community or (2) foreclose his or her freedom to take advantage of other employment opportunities by either (a) excluding him or her from a definite range of employment opportunities with the government or (b) broadly precluding him or her from continuing in his or her chosen career.[37] For an intelligence agency plaintiff, negatively altering his or her employment status by wrongly revoking a security clearance and, therefore, stigmatizing the employee so as to foreclose his or her freedom to take advantage of other employment opportunities, may well implicate a liberty interest.

In addition, a liberty interest may include the right not to be confronted with the purposeful destruction of one's standing and reputation in the community through false allegations and incrimination. False charges which purposely destroy an employee's standing and stigmatize that person within the

---

35. *Id.* at 1320.

36. *Dickson v. United States*, 831 F. Supp. 893, 898 (D.D.C. 1993).

37. *Siegert v. Gilley*, 500 U.S. 226, 233 (1991); *Codd v. Velger*, 429 U.S. 624, 627 (1977) (*per curiam*) (impugning statement must be substantially false); *Kartseva v. Dep't of State*, 37 F.3d 1524, 1527-8 (D.C. Cir. 1994); *United States Info. Agency v. Krc*, 905 F.2d 389, 397 (D.C. Cir. 1990). *See also Bd. of Regents v. Roth*, 408 U.S. 564, 573-74 (1978).

community could be the result of cover up, retaliation or revenge because, for example, a CIA employee reported wrongdoing or misconduct or criticized CIA policies or operations. This kind of personal destruction also could be the result of a biased CIA investigation instigated and/or perpetuated by federal officers who knew or should have known that the investigation was based on false allegations. Additionally, a liberty interests claim may involve unwarranted threats of criminal referral by the intelligence agency.

An intelligence agency plaintiff attempting to plead a claim based upon a Fifth Amendment due process liberty interest must meet a two-step test. First, the employee must allege harm to an interest greater than reputation.[38] Injury to reputation itself is not a liberty interest protected by the Constitution, and defamation is a tort. Consequently, the plaintiff needs to show that the false allegations made by other intelligence agency officers caused more than reputational damage, that these false accusations resulted, for example, in loss of present and future employment or loss of position within the community. Standing alone, dismissal or alteration in government employment status does not implicate a protected liberty interest.[39] Second, therefore, the plaintiff must allege that the other intelligence agency officers actually stigmatized his or her reputation to the point that the stigma hampered future prospects of gainful employment or regaining community standing. The stigma and the potential harm caused by being so stigmatized should be alleged with particularity.[40]

A case involving due process liberty interests which may be applicable to intelligence agency employees is *Kartseva v. Department of State*.[41] In *Kartseva*, an employee of a private contractor who performed government contract work as a Russian translator was fired. Although a State Department memorandum declared that she was ineligible for a security clearance due to "significant counterintelligence concerns raised during the conduct of background investigations…," no information on the content of those concerns was ever provided.[42] Kartseva asserted that the actions of the Government "interfered with her opportunity to obtain future employment in violation of…her due process rights under the Fifth Amendment to the United States Constitution."[43] The court held that Kartseva sufficiently pled a violation of her liberty interest to survive the Department of State's Motion to Dismiss. Additionally, the court stated:

---

38. *See supra* note 36, at 899.
39. *Bd. of Regents*, 408 U.S. at 575.
40. *See supra* note 36.
41. *Kartseva v. Dep't of State*, 37 F.3d 1524, 1527-8 (D.C. Cir. 1994).
42. *Id.* at 1525–26.
43. *Id.* at 1526–27.

Based on the present record and our precedents, there appear to be two ways in which State's action might have changed Kartseva's status and thus implicated a liberty interest. First, if State's action formally or automatically excludes Kartseva from work on some category of future State contracts or from other government employment opportunities, that action changes her formal legal status and thus implicates a liberty interest. Second, if State's action does not have this binding effect, but nevertheless has the broad effect of largely precluding Kartseva from pursuing her chosen career as a Russian translator, that, too, would constitute a "status change" adequate to implicate a liberty interest.[44]

Similarly, if intelligence agency defendants' willful and improper actions and omissions negatively alter an individual's employment status and, in doing so, impugn his or her reputation, seriously damaging the person's standing and associations in the community or foreclose his or her freedom to take advantage of other employment opportunities, a due process liberty interest is implicated. If the intelligence agency managers exclude an employee from a definite range of employment opportunities, their action changes his or her employment status and has a binding negative effect. Also, if the intelligence agency's action largely precludes an individual from pursuing his or her chosen career, that too constitutes a negative status change and involves a liberty interest.

3. Procedural Due Process

In addition to substantive Fifth Amendment rights, an intelligence agency employee has certain procedural due process guarantees. The Due Process Clause requires procedural due process only where an employee is deprived of a protected liberty or property interest.[45] Procedural due process rights are implicated if an employee is blocked by other intelligence agency officers from resorting to internal administrative remedies, if administrative proceedings are wrongfully initiated against an employee without proper notice, or if ad-

---

44. *Id.* at 1527–28. *See also Taylor v. Resolution Trust Corp.*, 56 F.3d 1497, 1506 (D.C. Cir. 1995) (concluding that government action infringes constitutionally protected liberty interests even when preclusion from future employment opportunities is broad), *and Mc Knight v. Southeastern Pa. Transp. Auth.*, 583 F.2d 1229, 1236 (3d Cir. 1978) (holding that harm to future employment possibilities may show sufficient stigma to allow a claim for a violation of a liberty interest).

45. *Bd. of Regents*, 408 U.S. at 569–70.

verse administrative decisions are wrongfully taken against an employee without an adequate hearing. Procedural due process rights also may be violated if required internal remedies exist on paper, but in reality are pretextual or, worse, function as roadblocks by which managers delay and block an employee from taking civil action in court. An Office of Equal Employment Opportunity (OEEO) which decides against the complainant in over 98 percent of the cases and manipulates and obstructs internal administrative processing, as does the CIA's OEEO, appears to fit into such a pretextual mold.[46]

4. Equal Protection Rights

Other constitutional rights which an intelligence agency employee, including a CIA officer, has or should have are the rights to equal protection under the laws and to be free from illegal discrimination. In *Doe v. Gates*, however, Doe argued for an equal protection right but did not prevail.[47] Doe claimed that because of the CIA's blanket policy against homosexuals, his employment was terminated in violation of the constitutional guarantee of equal protection.[48] The court said that the government would prevail in its summary judgment motion if the evidence showed Doe's employment was terminated on a basis unrelated to the alleged policy against homosexuals or because no such policy existed.[49] First, the court found no evidence of a blanket policy against homosexuals.[50] It noted, however, that even if there were such a policy, Doe would not be able to recover unless he established that his termination was the result of that policy.[51] Second, the court determined that the CIA discharged Doe because his homosexual conduct was a threat to national security, not because of a policy against homosexuals.[52] Consequently, it granted the government's motion for summary judgment on the grounds that the plaintiff had failed to demonstrate any issue of material fact which would allow his equal protection claim to stand.[53]

---

46. According to an OEEO counselor who requested anonymity, the CIA's OEEO decides against the complainant in over 98 percent of the cases. The CIA's OEEO is supposed to file these statistics with EEOC annually (*See also* Chapter Four, Section F, note 104).

47. *See supra* note 35.

48. Doe could not bring suit for employment discrimination under to Title VII because this statute does not include homosexuals as a federally protected group.

49. *See supra* note 35, at 1322.

50. *Id.*

51. *Id.* at 1324.

52. *Id.*

53. *Id.*

As this case demonstrates, an equal protection claim may be difficult to prove against a secret agency such as the CIA. First, if it has a policy against homosexuals or a protected group, the policy would be unwritten. Second, probably no CIA manager in a position to know would commit career suicide by testifying to the existence of such a blanket policy. Third, the CIA can always come up with a pretext for firing an employee, as it appears to have done in *Doe*, where the CIA claimed he was terminated for legitimate security interests.

In an equal protection case, the plaintiff needs to show that intelligence agency managers applied regulations and/or laws to him or her unequally, unreasonably or inequitably. The litigant must establish that he or she was treated differently than other employees and that there was no reasonable basis for doing so.

5. First Amendment Rights

Although an intelligence agency employee's constitutional guarantees to freedom of the press and speech may be circumscribed by his or her secrecy agreement with the agency, the employee still should possess the First Amendment rights to assemble and to petition the government for redress of grievances. An intelligence agency employee similarly should have the right to criticize the agency's wrongful policies, practices and operations. In addition, he or she must have a channel through which to report without fear of reprisal misconduct within the agency or illegal undertakings. Clearly, an individual should have the right to express disagreement with adverse personnel actions taken against him or her. If an intelligence agency employee's criticisms, reports of misconduct or disagreements are discouraged and chilled, he or she may have a First Amendment claim under *Bivens*, despite the secrecy agreement.[54]

D. Heightened Pleading Standard

The government has also argued for a "heightened pleading" standard in *Bivens* cases. This standard has been accepted in the District of Columbia Circuit, where the plaintiff charges a government official with a constitutional deprivation based on the official's state of mind, intent or motive.[55] The

---

54. *Kotarski v. Cooper*, 799 F.2d 1342 (9th Cir. 1986).
55. *Kimberlin v. Quinlan*, 303 U.S. App. D.C. 330 (1993); 6 F.3d 789, 793–94 (D.C. Cir. 1993).

Supreme Court, however, rejected this heightened pleading standard in civil rights cases against municipal officials under 42 U.S.C. § 1983 and noted it had not considered whether individual government officials entitled to qualified immunity required a heightened pleading standard.[56] The Court added, however, that a heightened pleading standard applied to a motion to dismiss based only on the pleading could not be reconciled with the liberal system of 'notice pleading' established by the Federal Rules of Civil Procedure. The Federal Rules require that a complaint include only a short and plain statement of the claim, the grounds upon which it is based and an averment that the plaintiff is entitled to relief.[57]

Nonetheless, when making a *Bivens* claim against an intelligence agency defendant, the plaintiff and counsel should make every effort to set forth the claims with as much specificity as possible. Identify the clearly established constitutional right which was violated, how that right was violated and what actions were taken by intelligence agency officers to violate that interest.

E. Preclusion

A *Bivens* action does not appear to have a preclusive effect on other claims being pursued separately or simultaneously, nor do other claims preempt *Bivens*. Courts, in fact, have recognized the importance of guaranteeing constitutional rights, especially since *Bivens* may have some advantages over other legal claims. *Bivens*, the courts have pointed out, has a deterrent value.[58] It allows for punitive damages as well as awards for other injuries, including mental and emotional distress.[59] It provides the option of a jury trial.[60] Importantly, it is not limited to actions available under state law.[61]

The Supreme Court in *Carlson* examined the question of preclusion. Specifically, it asked whether a *Bivens* remedy would be available even though the allegations also could support a suit against the United States under the Federal Tort Claims Act (FTCA).[62] *Bivens*, the Court noted, could be defeated

---

56. *Leatherman v. Tarrant County Narcotics Intelligence & Coordination Unit*, 507 U.S. 163 (1993).

57. *Id.* at 168.

58. *See supra* note 27, at 21.

59. *Id.* at 22.

60. *Id.*

61. *Id.* at 15; *also supra* note 24, at 676.

62. *Id. Carlson* at 16.

only in two situations: first, "when the defendants demonstrate special factors counseling hesitation in the absence of affirmative action by Congress"[63] and, second, "when defendants show that Congress has provided an alternative remedy which it explicitly declared to be a substitute for recovery directly under the Constitution and viewed as equally effective."[64]

Regarding the first point, the Court decided that the federal defendants in *Carlson* did not enjoy any status in our constitutional scheme to suggest that judicially created remedies against them could be inappropriate.[65] It found, instead, that the qualified immunity accorded to them was adequate protection.[66] Second, the Court did not find that Congress had provided any explicit substitute for *Bivens* or a remedy as equally effective as that provided in *Bivens*.[67] On the contrary, the Court said:

> [W]hen Congress amended the FTCA in 1974 to create a cause of action against the United States for intentional torts committed by federal law enforcement officers, the Congressional comments accompanying that amendment made it crystal clear that Congress views the FTCA and Bivens as parallel, complementary causes of action.... [I]nnocent individuals...will have a cause of action against individual Federal agents and the Federal Government. Furthermore, this provision should be viewed as a counterpart to the Bivens case and its progeny (sic), in that it waives the defense of sovereign immunity so as to make the Government independently liable in damages for the same type of conduct that is alleged to have occurred in Bivens.... In the absence of a contrary expression from Congress, [the FTCA] contemplates that victims of the kind of... wrongdoing alleged in this complaint shall have an action under the FTCA against the United States as well as a Bivens action against individual officials alleged to have infringed their constitutional rights.[68]

The court in *Grichenko* supported this conclusion, noting that the plaintiff's action for denial of procedural due process was separate from his sub-

---

63. *Id.* at 18.
64. *Id.* at 18–19.
65. *Id.* at 19.
66. *Id.*
67. *Id.*
68. *Id.* at 18–19.

stantive claim of an eye injury.[69] It said that while the FECA was the plaintiff's exclusive remedy against the United States in seeking compensation for an eye injury, it did not provide an available, or substitute, remedy for the constitutional violations he asserted.[70] Whether the plaintiff would prevail on the substantive merits of the compensation claim was irrelevant to the *Bivens* cause of action.[71]

Similarly in *Kotarski v. Cooper*, the government argued that Title VII and *Bush v. Lucas*[72] precluded Kotarski's *Bivens* claim.[73] Kotarski, a civilian Navy engineer, had been promoted to a supervisory position subject to a one-year period of probation. Upon learning that he would be returned to his prior position, he filed a civil action seeking reinstatement, back pay and *Bivens* damages for his demotion.[74] Kotarski alleged that he was demoted as retaliation for his expression of disagreement with certain naval policies, practices and expenditures in violation of his First Amendment rights and for participating in an employment discrimination complaint filed by a woman friend.[75]

The court in *Kotarski* acknowledged the federal government's argument that *Brown v. General Services Administration* held that Title VII was the exclusive remedy for claims of discrimination in federal employment. It explained, however, that this exclusion extends only to claims of federal employees cognizable under Title VII. Discrimination claims do not preempt separate remedies for unconstitutional conduct.[76]

The court also recognized that in *Bush*, the Supreme Court rejected a *Bivens* claim of a non-probationary federal employee who alleged his demotion was a reprisal for a constitutionally protected activity, because Congress had already established an elaborate regulatory and remedial scheme governing federal employer-employee relationships.[77] The court here distinguished *Kotarski*, however, for three reasons. First, the primary interest which Kotarski asserted was a First Amendment right of free speech. Second, it was essential to the Supreme Court in *Bush* that a meaningful remedy for an alleged constitutional violation was available. Third, the remedies available under the Civil Service

---

69. *See supra* note 24, at 674.
70. *Id.* at 677.
71. *Id.*
72. *Bush v. Lucas*, 462 U.S. 367 (1983).
73. *See supra* note 54.
74. *Id.* at 1344.
75. *Id.* at 1345.
76. *Id.*
77. *Id.* at 1346.

Reform Act (CSRA) to employees in a probationary status were not adequate within the meaning of *Bush*.[78]

The court reasoned that probationary status could not be the foundation for a total negation of an individual's First Amendment rights.[79] Guided by *Bush* then, it examined whether the Congressional and administrative remedies which Kotarski possessed as a probationary employee were sufficient to provide meaningful protection to his constitutional rights.[80] The court found that even if a probationary employee demonstrated a constitutional violation, he or she had no right to participate in any investigative and decision-making process determining whether to take action, no enforceable right, no judicial review and no meaningful remedies.[81]

In reaching its conclusion the court said:

> The defendants contend that it is anomalous to give probationary employees a greater protection of their constitutional rights, by way of a Bivens action, than is available to fully tenured employees, who are confined to their civil service remedies. It may be. The alternative, which strikes us as at least equally anomalous, is to hold that a Bivens action that would otherwise be appropriate for a probationary employee is rendered inappropriate by the enactment of a scheme of enforceable remedies from which probationary employees are excluded by definition. To reach such a result, we would have to conclude that Congress had both the intention and the authority to deprive probationary employees of all meaningful protection for their constitutional rights.[82]

The court held that Kotarski, as a probationary supervisor, is not preempted by *Bush* from pursuing a *Bivens* action.[83]

Applying *Kotarski* to the CIA, as well as other intelligence agencies, Agency plaintiffs may well have First Amendment constitutional claims when other employees take retaliatory steps against them for expressing disagreement with certain policies, practices and procedures, reporting wrongdoing and misconduct or petitioning the court or elected government officials for a redress of grievances. Intelligence agency officials also may violate and be sued for the

---

78. *Id.* at 1346–47.
79. *Id.* at 1347.
80. *Id.*
81. *Id.* at 1348.
82. *Id.* at 1349.
83. *Id.* at 1350.

denial of other constitutional rights, including substantive and procedural due process guarantees pursuant to the Fifth Amendment and unlawful searches and seizures under the Fourth Amendment. As in *Kotarski*, CIA employees are not included in any of the systematic and comprehensive remedial reforms provided under the CSRA, nor do they possess any other real internal remedies should their constitutional rights be violated by other federal officers. CIA officers, in fact, generally are denied any meaningful participation in investigative and decision-making processes which result in adverse personnel actions being taken against them. They have few, if any, enforceable rights or avenues for relief. It seems unlikely, therefore, that Agency employees would be barred from filing a *Bivens* claim for unconstitutional acts to which they are subjected by federal officials acting under the color of law.[84]

F. Statute of Limitations

A state's personal injury statute of limitations generally provides the applicable time limit for filing a *Bivens* claim, whether in state court or district court. Since state law supplies the statute of limitations in *Bivens* actions, time limits vary from state-to-state, and attorneys must research this issue early on. In Washington, D.C. the time for bringing an action for recovery for personal injuries, and therefore for *Bivens*, is three years from the time the right to maintain the action began to accrue.[85] In Virginia, the statute of limitations is two years,[86] and in Maryland, it is three.[87] In some states, such as California, the statute of limitation is as short as one year.

---

84. *See also* Chapter Three, Section A for the argument that the Supreme Court's decision in *United States v. Fausto*, 484 U.S. 439 (1988), should not be applicable to CIA employees who are non-civil service federal government employees, not covered by the CSRA. There are no special factors counseling hesitation for CIA employees because Congress has provided no alternative remedy.

85. D.C. Code Ann. § 12-301(8) (1998).

86. Va. Code Ann. § 8.01-243(A) (Michie 1992).

87. Md. Code Ann. Cts. & Jud. Proc. § 5-101.

CHAPTER SEVEN

EMPLOYMENT-RELATED CIVIL CONSPIRACIES

This Chapter and the next examine the applicability of civil conspiracy statutes to suits against intelligence agencies for causes of action involving illegal adverse personnel action conspiracies. The analysis initially addresses three subsections of 42 U.S.C. §1985: conspiracy to interfere with the performance of official duties by a federal officer—42 U.S.C. §1985(1); conspiracy to obstruct justice—42 U.S.C. §1985(2); and conspiracy to deprive a person of equal protection and equal privileges and immunities—42 U.S.C. §1985 (3). Case law provides some answers to the question whether or not federal actors can be sued under this statute and, if so, what types of conspiratorial conduct would be actionable. Following this discussion, a brief explanation is given about 42 U.S.C. §1986, a damage remedy available to the extent a 42 U.S.C. §1985 claim succeeds. Damages, not injunctive relief, are available under this statute.

Since the approach of the Supreme Court to these statutes is to accord them a "sweep as broad as their language,"[1] 42 U.S.C. §1985 (1), (2), and (3) are interpreted broadly here. Consistent with the Supreme Court's intent, some lower courts have construed 42 U.S.C. §1985 to encompass and create substantive rights not found elsewhere.[2]

Chapter Eight also looks at civil conspiracy, examining the interesting question of whether a civil RICO action could be taken against colluding intelligence agency officers who commit two or more predicate acts in connection with the conduct of an enterprise which injures another employee in his or her business or property.[3] Although litigating against CIA officials under civil RICO is a new concept, the Supreme Court's broad interpretation of the

---

1. *Griffin v. Breckenridge*, 403 U.S. 88, 97 (1971).

2. *Kenna v. United States Dep't of Justice*, 727 F. Supp. 64, 73-74 (D.C.N.H. 1989).

3. Civil Racketeer Influenced and Corrupt Organizations Act (RICO), 18 U.S.C.A. §§1961, 1962, 1964 (West 2000).

statute suggests that the actions of some CIA officers may well come within RICO's reach. If evidence points to certain unlawful conspiratorial conduct by intelligence agency officials, it may be worth a try to include a RICO count in the plaintiff's complaint, especially if the civil RICO claim is pursued concurrently with more traditional avenues of relief.

A. Unlawful Conspiracy Defined

"Conspiracy" is a combination or confederacy between two or more persons formed for the purpose of committing, by joint efforts, some unlawful act, or some act which is lawful in itself, but becomes unlawful when done by the concerted action of the conspirators.[4] The main element in a conspiracy is the agreement among parties to inflict a wrong or an injury on another person.[5]

The participants in the conspiracy share a general conspiratorial objective, but they need not know all the details of the plan or possess exactly the same motives as the other conspirators.[6] In the case *Windsor v. Tennessean*, for instance, motives included personal dislike and fear.[7]

A conspiracy usually is "not born full grown" but emerges in successive stages. During its growth and development, it often becomes necessary to bring in certain parties. The agreement, therefore, may not be made among all the parties at the same time.[8]

Since illegal conspiracies rarely are evidenced by explicit agreements, the plaintiff generally must rely on circumstantial evidence and reasonable inferences to prove his or her case.[9] Essentially, it would be open to a jury, in the light of the sequence of events, to infer from the circumstances that there existed the necessary "meeting of the minds" to form an unlawful conspiracy.[10]

---

4. *Black's Law Dictionary Abridged*, 214 (6th ed. 1994).

5. *Bell v. City of Milwaukee*, 746 F.2d 1205, 1255 (7th Cir. 1984).

6. *Id.* at 1259.

7. *Windsor v. Tennessean*, 719 F.2d 155, 160 (6th Cir. 1983), *reh'g denied*, 726 F.2d 277 (6th Cir. 1984).

8. *Blumenthal v. United States*, 332 U.S. 539, 556 (1947).

9. *Way v. Mueller Brass Co.*, 840 F.2d 303, 308 (5th Cir. 1988).

10. *Adickes v. Kress Co.*, 398 U.S. 144, 158 (1970).

B. Adverse Personnel Actions within U.S. Intelligence May Take Form of Unlawful Conspiracies

Conspiratorial conduct is a commonplace phenomenon within intelligence agencies. The CIA, with its penchant for secrecy and the targeting of its prey, provides a fertile ground for conspiracies to develop and flourish. It is hardly inconceivable that two or more CIA officials could agree and unlawfully act in concert to inflict harm upon a fellow employee. The injury resulting from such conspiratorial conduct may manifest itself as an adverse personnel action such as giving the victim a poor evaluation or forcing him or her to resign or assume a lesser position. Particularly egregious would be the exploitation of clandestine operational skills by trained intelligence agency operatives to support unlawful personnel actions against a colleague.

An intelligence agency conspiracy may be confined to one office, but more often it appears to involve officials in two or three separate components. The CIA's Office of the Inspector General (OIG), for example, could unlawfully collude with managers of the Office of Medical Services (OMS) and the Office of Equal Employment Opportunity (OEEO).[11] Hence, when an employee files a discrimination complaint, reports wrongdoing and/or becomes the target of an OIG investigation, the party also may find that OMS has conducted an "indirect psychological assessment" and placed a medical hold on him or her, without so much as an interview.[12]

If a CIA employee tries to obtain relief, all internal avenues of redress generally close. The complainant likely will be ostracized and faced with concealment and cover-up of relevant evidence and witnesses. There is no meaningful investigation, no real due process, no hearing, no identification of evidence or witnesses and no ability to confront accusers. CIA managers, aware of the collusion and conspiracy and in a position to prevent it, usually choose to stay out of harm's way and thus turn their backs on the victim.

If adverse personnel actions interfere with the performance of the employee's duties, obstruct justice and/or deprive an individual of equal protection and equal privileges and immunities under the law, the aggrieved party may well have a case pursuant to the civil right conspiracy statutes. The plain-

---

11. *See* Chapter One, Section B.1. on Collusion, Retaliation, and Reprisals.
12. *See* Actual CIA Cases—*Betty*, case B; *Doris*, case E; *Hannah*, case H; *Jill*, case J.

tiff then needs to focus on establishing, at least circumstantially, the elements of a cause of action for conspiracy.

C. Analysis of Civil Conspiracy Statutes: 42 U.S.C. 1985 §§ (1), (2), and (3), and 42 U.S.C 1986

Despite the fact that until the last twenty years, 42 U.S.C. § 1985 was a little-used nineteenth-century civil rights statute, legal precedent now exists for federal government employees to sue other United States officials allegedly responsible for employment-related conspiracies under one or more of 42 U.S.C. § 1985's three distinct subsections. Generally, however, defendants have contended that these allegations fail to state a claim upon which relief can be granted because 42 U.S.C. § 1985 does not apply to defendants who are acting as federal employees. This argument often has proven to be specious.

1. Conspiracy to Interfere with Performance of Official Duties by Federal Officer {42 U.S.C. § 1985(1)}

Subsection 42 U.S.C. § 1985(1) proscribes conspiracies that interfere with the performance of official duties by federal officers.[13] Specifically, a cause of action exists under 42 U.S.C. § 1985(1):

> If *two or more persons* in any State or Territory *conspire to prevent...* any person from accepting or holding any office, trust, or place of confidence under the United States, or *from discharging any duties* thereof; *or to injure him* in his person or property *on account of his lawful discharge of the duties of his office, or while engaged in the lawful discharge thereof... or impede him in the discharge of his official duties* (emphasis added).

Since 1978, in response to the federal government's argument that 42 U.S.C. § 1985(1) does not apply to federal actors, numerous cases have addressed this issue and several courts have found that U.S. government officials may be liable for conspiracy under this subsection. These cases also provide some examples of types of adverse employment measures that are actionable under the civil rights conspiracy statutes.

---

13. *Kush v. Rutledge*, 460 U.S. 719, 724 (1983).

One of the early cases, *Perry v. Golub*, involved a federal officer who was employed as the Deputy Director of Birmingham's District Equal Employment Opportunity Commission (EEOC).[14] Perry alleged that his superiors arbitrarily and without the prerequisite procedural safeguards ordered him permanently reassigned because he protested and eventually reported irregularities in EEOC's handling of cases. After a preliminary hearing, the district court found a substantial likelihood that the plaintiff would prevail on the merits of one or more of his claims. Specifically, it held that pursuant to 42 U.S.C. § 1985(1) "the permanent reassignment constituted an attempt to prevent him (the plaintiff) from discharging the duties of his office or to injure him in his person or property on account of the lawful discharge of the duties of his office."[15] *Perry v. Golub* demonstrated that a federal actor indeed could be sued under this civil rights conspiracy statute and that an adverse employment action such as permanent reassignment could interfere with a federal officer's performance of his official duties and, therefore, be legally actionable.

Three years later, in *Stith v. Tanner*, the district court stated unequivocally that 42 U.S.C. § 1985(1) would apply where defendants, acting as federal employees, were participating in a conspiracy proscribed by the subsection.[16] Analyzing the origins of 42 U.S.C. § 1985(1) in order to interpret its applicability to federal defendants, the court suggested that the most likely source of constitutional authority for this subsection would be the Necessary and Proper Clause, United States Constitution, Art. I, Section 8.[17] Consequently, it concluded there would be no constitutional infirmity in construing 42 U.S.C. § 1985(1) to include defendants who were acting as federal employees.[18] In this case, however, which involved an employee discharged from the Department of Housing and Urban Development, the court found his claim to be strictly one of racial discrimination based on his advocacy of improved treatment of racial minorities.[19]

In *Lawrence v. Acree*, the plaintiff, a Regional Commissioner of the United States Customs Service, sued his former colleagues for unlawfully conspiring to force him to resign, retire or otherwise relinquish his position.[20] The United States Court of Appeals assumed *arguendo* for the purposes of deciding an of-

---

14. *Perry v. Golub*, 400 F. Supp. 409 (N.D. Ala. 1975).
15. *Id.* at 411, 417.
16. *Stith v. Tanner*, 447 F. Supp. 970, 973-74 (M.D.N.C. 1978).
17. *Id.* at 973.
18. *Id.*
19. *Id.* at 974.
20. *Lawrence v. Acree*, 665 F.2d. 1319 (D.C. Cir. 1981).

ficial immunity claim that a 42 U.S.C. §1985(1) action would ordinarily lie against federal officials.[21] The court also agreed with the plaintiff that Congress did not preempt an action under 42 U.S.C. §1985(1) with the limited remedy it provided under the Performance Rating Act.[22] The court suggested, in fact, that a performance evaluation may be one element of an actionable conspiracy.[23]

Lawrence v. Acree could be important legal precedent for an intelligence agency plaintiff because the case was heard before the United States Court of Appeals, D.C. Circuit. A civil action brought by an intelligence agency employee, particularly a CIA officer, could well be filed in the District of Columbia and, therefore, this case precedent would be authoritative. Here the court assumed that the civil rights conspiracy statutes were actionable against federal actors and suggested performance appraisals could be an element of a conspiracy. Within the CIA, one of the conspiratorial steps taken against employees, according to reports from those listed above in Actual CIA Cases, is giving a complainant a marginal evaluation.

Mollow v. Carlton involved a pilot in the United States Air Force and Air Force Reserve who alleged conspiracy by various of his commanding officers to suppress his reports about the unsafe conditions and policies in the operation of heavy jet aircraft. According to his complaint, an aircraft subsequently crashed in precisely the manner he had predicted, which resulted in his superiors having him imprisoned in a psychiatric ward to prevent him from testifying about the crash.[24] Here the court noted that 42 U.S.C. §1985(1) is legislation specifically authorizing a suit by an injured federal officer against his superiors.[25] Nonetheless, it concluded that military subordinates do not have a remedy under this subsection against their military superiors.[26]

Mollow v. Carlton is significant to an intelligence agency employee-litigant for two reasons. It suggests that superiors who agree to take action against an employee for reporting wrongful governmental policies and procedures may be opening themselves up to a suit for unlawful conspiracy. *Mollow* also reenforced the point that federal officials were not immune under 42 U.S.C. §1985(1). It noted, in fact, that litigation against individual federal officers by the injured party was specifically authorized by the statute.

---

21. *Id.* at 1322.
22. *Id.* at 1323.
23. *Id.*
24. *Mollow v. Carlton*, 716 F.2d 627, 628 (9th Cir. 1983).
25. *Id.* at 630–31.
26. *Id.*

Two additional cases, *Windsor v. Tennessean* and *Kenna v. United States Department of Justice*, demonstrate the courts' efforts to comply with the Supreme Court's urging that the civil rights conspiracy statutes be given a very broad sweep. The decisions indicate just how far 42 U.S.C. § 1985(1) may go to create rights for victims who sue federal officials.

In *Windsor*, where a former Assistant United States Attorney sued a former United States Attorney and several newspaper employees to recover for damages arising out of his dismissal from federal employment, the court agreed with the plaintiff that a conspiracy to harm a federal officer's reputation because of or while engaged in the lawful discharge of his duties was actionable under 42 U.S.C. § 1985(1).[27] Windsor alleged that the defendants had conspired to print defamatory articles about him for the purpose of obtaining his dismissal. In its opinion, the Court pointed out that construing 42 U.S.C. § 1985(1) to encompass Windsor's complaint was consistent with the Supreme Court's approach to accord the civil rights statutes a broad sweep.[28] The court noted also that this statute provided only for damages, not injunctive relief or restatement of employment.[29]

Nonetheless, although *Windsor* stated a cause of action under 42 U.S.C. § 1985(1), the court held that a reasonable person would not have known in 1980 that an agreement to defame a federal officer in order to effect his discharge violated this subsection.[30] Hence, since the former United States attorney did not transgress any clearly established federal statutory right, he was granted qualified immunity. The court warned that "[s]imilar violations by federal officials or employees will, however, be actionable in the future."[31]

In *Kenna v. United States Department of Justice*, the court traced the purpose of 42 U.S.C. § 1985 and made an important pronouncement regarding the substantive rights which the statute created.[32] Here, when a former Assistant United States Attorney sued seeking reinstatement and damages for wrongful dismissal, the court summed up legal precedents on the issue of whether a federal government employee could sue a superior under 42 U.S.C. § 1985(1).[33] It recognized that although the original purpose of the statute was to protect federal officials responsible for implementing reconstruction in the post Civil War

---

27. *See supra* note 7, at 157.
28. *Id.* at 161.
29. *Id.* at 160.
30. *Id.* at 165.
31. *Id.*
32. *See supra* note 2.
33. *Id.* at 73–4.

South, 42 U.S.C. §1985's reach had been extended well beyond that goal.[34] The court noted the intention of the Supreme Court to give this statute a very broad sweep. Further, the court said 42 U.S.C. §1985 did more than other civil rights statutes in that it created substantive rights not found elsewhere.[35] Accordingly in some circumstances, the court concluded that 42 U.S.C. §1985 (1) had permitted a federal official to bring suit against a superior who unlawfully conspired to cause his discharge or deny him a promotion.[36]

The opinion pointed out, however, that the statute was not a vehicle for challenging every adverse employment decision regarding a federal government employee. The essence of the proscribed conduct under 42 U.S.C. §1985(1) was that the defendants were acting with the intent to impede the employee in properly performing his or her official duties.[37]

In view of the case law involving employees suing their federal government supervisors for employment-related conspiracy actions, it is conceivable that an intelligence agency employee could bring a civil action against other intelligence agency officials for conspiring to prevent him or her from performing his official duties. Importantly, as noted in *Kenna*, 42 U.S.C. §1985 created substantive rights not found elsewhere. Consequently, although the government cannot be held accountable for libel, slander or loss of reputation under the Federal Tort Claims Act, per *Windsor*, an employee may be able to sue pursuant to 42 U.S.C. §1985(1) for a conspiracy to harm his or her reputation while engaged in the lawful discharge of his duties as a federal officer. Wrongful dismissal, denial of promotion, poor performance evaluations, permanent reassignment, forced resignation and retaliation and reprisal for reporting wrongdoing also may be actionable against intelligence agency officials who unlawfully conspire against an employee. Under these civil rights conspiracy statutes, the plaintiff may be awarded damages, but he or she will not obtain injunctive relief or reemployment, if terminated.

2. Conspiracy to Obstruct Justice {42 U.S.C. §1985(2)}

Subsection 42 U.S.C. §1985(2) is aimed at conspiracies that obstruct justice. Under it, a cause of action exists:

---

34. *Id.* at 73.
35. *Id.*
36. *Id.*
37. *Id.* at 74.

If two or more persons conspire for the purpose of impeding, hindering, obstructing, or defeating, in any manner, the due course of justice...with the intent to deny any citizen the equal protection of the laws, or to injure him or his property for lawfully enforcing, or attempting to enforce, the right of any person, or class of persons, to the equal protection of the laws.

In *Kush v. Rutledge*, a suit was brought by a white football player who alleged conspiracy to obstruct justice through the intimidation of potential witnesses in a federal lawsuit.[38] The petitioners argued for dismissal on the grounds that there was no claim that the conspiracy was motivated by racial or class-based, invidiously discriminatory animus.

Justice Stevens, who gave the opinion of the court, traced the history of 42 U.S.C. § 1985 to its origins in section two of the Civil Rights Act of 1871, 17 Stat. 13, and then analyzed and interpreted each subsection. He noted that 42 U.S.C. § 1985(2) concerned the administration of justice and the protection of the processes of the courts.[39] This subsection of the statute prohibited the intimidation of parties, witnesses and jurors in federal court. Justice Stevens pointed out that no allegations of racial or class-based, invidiously discriminatory animus were required to establish a cause of action for conspiracy to interfere with the administration of justice.[40]

Hence an intelligence agency employee, without having to allege discriminatory animus, may have a cause of action under 42 U.S.C. § 1985(2) for an adverse personnel action where certain agency defendants conspire to deliberately impede justice. Obstruction of justice by intelligence agency conspirators could take the form of the destruction or concealment of evidence, the intimidation or concealment of potential witnesses, false statements, fabrications and cover-up.

3. Conspiracy to Deprive Person of Equal Protection and Equal Privileges and Immunities {42 U.S.C. § 1985(3)}

Subsection 42 U.S.C. § 1985(3) is the subsection that addresses conspiracy motivated by racial or class-based animus. It proscribes a conspiracy to deprive any person of his or her rights and privileges or equal protection under the law. Under 42 U.S.C. § 1985(3), a plaintiff has a cause of action:

---

38. *See supra* note 13, at 719.
39. *Id.* at 727.
40. *Id.* at 721.

> If two or more persons in any State or Territory conspire...for the purpose of depriving, either directly or indirectly, any person or class of persons of equal protection of the laws, or of equal privileges and immunities under the law....In any case of conspiracy set forth in this section, if one or more persons engaged therein do, or cause to be done, any act in furtherance of the object of such conspiracy, whereby another is injured in his person or property, or deprived of having and exercising any right or privilege of a citizen of the United States, the party so injured or deprived may have action for recovery of damages occasioned by such injury or deprivations, against any one or more of the conspirators.

Over one hundred years ago, Justice Harlan, giving the opinion of the Supreme Court in *United States v. Harris*, interpreted this subsection of the statute broadly, noting it was Congressional intent in section 1985(3) to speak of all deprivations of equal protection of the laws and equal privileges and immunities under the laws.[41]

A good example of a 42 U.S.C. § 1985(3) case was *Bell v. City of Milwaukee*, which concerned government officials, acting under the authority of the law, who conspired to deprive the family of a slain black male of its constitutional right to equal protection of the laws.[42] Here, employees of the city of Milwaukee, involved in the investigation of the killing of a young man by a co-worker, conspired to conceal facts and evidence and obstructed legitimate efforts to seek judicial redress, interfering with the plaintiffs' due process right of access to the courts.[43] The defendants portrayed their actions as the natural product of the adversarial system. The court, however, refused to countenance so gross a distortion of the facts. It pointed out that this cover-up and resistance by the conspirators perpetuated the wrong and rendered hollow the plaintiffs' right to judicial redress, protected under 42 U.S.C. §§ 1985(2) and 1985(3).[44]

Assessing the allegations in a 42 U.S.C. § 1985(3) complaint in *Azar v. Conley*, the court discussed the requirement for invidiously discriminatory animus.[45] It noted that the statute forbids any conspiracy for the purpose of depriving a person or class of persons of equal protection of the laws.[46] Although

---

41. *United States v. Harris*, 106 U.S. 629, 643 (1883).
42. *See supra* note 5, at 1260, 1262.
43. *Id.* at 1261.
44. *Id.*
45. *Azar v. Conley*, 456 F.2d 1382, 1385 (6th Cir. 1972).
46. *Id.*

in this case the plaintiffs asserting the civil rights action were members of a white middle class family, the court found that the Azars had adequately alleged the requisite mental state of invidiously discriminatory animus to assert a cause of action under 42 U.S.C. § 1985(3).[47] One does not have to be a woman, a person of color or a member of any minority group to meet the requirement for invidiously discriminatory animus.

In a suit under 42 U.S.C. § 1985 against conspiring intelligence agency officers, the plaintiff need not be a member of a certain minority group to show discriminatory animus. Evidence of harassment, intimidation, reprisals, concealment of evidence and witnesses and cover-up by colluding intelligence agency managers should be enough to establish the requisite mental state for discriminatory animus.

The question whether a federal employee may sue other federal employees for conspiracy under 42 U.S.C. § 1985(3), as well as under 42 U.S.C. § 1985(1), was also addressed by the *Stith* court. The district court allowed that there were some decisions which held that 42 U.S.C. § 1985(3) did not apply where defendants were acting as federal officers.[48] It noted, however, that these decisions were apparently premised on the notion that this subsection was grounded in the Fourteenth Amendment and that action under color of state law was essential for liability under 42 U.S.C. § 1985(3).[49] The court pointed out that no where in the text of this subsection was there any indication that the defendant must be acting under the color of any law, state or federal. The court then mentioned the rejection of the requirement for state action in *Griffin*, at least, where racial discrimination was involved.[50] It added that the Supreme Court in *Griffin* held that 42 U.S.C. § 1985(3) was aimed at all conspiracies which deprived persons of certain federally protected rights.[51] The court concluded that given the Supreme Court's decision in *Griffin* and the plain language of 42 U.S.C. § 1985(3), this subsection would apply to federal defendants who participated in a conspiracy that would otherwise be proscribed under this statute.[52] Hence, it would seem that CIA employees similarly could have a cause of action against other federal government officials for conspiracy to deprive them of equal protection and equal privileges and immunities under this subsection.

---

47. *Id.*
48. *See supra* note 16, at 972.
49. *Id.* at 972–73.
50. *Id.*; *see also supra* note 1, at 91.
51. *Id.*
52. *Id.*

There is also a damage element in 42 U.S.C. § 1985(3). If the allegations are proven, an injured party may recover damages occasioned by the injury or deprivation from any one or more of the conspirators. The conspirators shall be fined not more than $5,000 or imprisoned not more than ten years or both.[53]

4. Damage Remedy against Those with Knowledge of Conspiracy, Power to Prevent It, but Who Neglect or Refuse to Do So (42 U.S.C. § 1986)

Section 42 U.S.C. § 1986 provides a damage remedy against those who had knowledge of a type of conspiracy mentioned under 42 U.S.C. § 1985 above and the power to stop it, but did not. This section is only available to the extent there is a cause of action under 42 U.S.C. § 1985 and, in fact, serves to bolster the protection afforded by that subsection.[54] Specifically, the statute states:

> Every person who, having knowledge that any of the wrongs conspired to be done, and mentioned in section 1985 of this title, are about to be committed, and having power to prevent or aid in preventing the commission of the same, neglects or refuses so to do, if such wrongful act be committed, shall be liable to the party injured, or his legal representatives, for all damages caused by such wrongful acts, which such person by reasonable diligence could have prevented; and such damages may be recovered in an action on the case; and any number of persons guilty of such wrongful neglect or refusal may be joined as defendants in the action....

Section 42 U.S.C. § 1986 would be particularly applicable to those intelligence agency managers who are aware that a conspiracy is in process which will deprive another employee of his or her rights under the Constitution and federal law, have the power to prevent it, but turn a blind eye. Many in the CIA are loathe to speak up to try to stop wrongdoing, fearing they will be implicated or victimized. Moreover, Agency officials generally fear airing their dirty laundry before the Senate or House Intelligence Committees, the Department of Justice or the courts. If CIA officers were made aware that liabil-

---

53. *See supra* note 1, at 98 n.4.
54. *Robeson v. Fanella*, 94 F. Supp. 62 (S.D.N.Y. 1950).

ity under 42 U.S.C. §1986 is derivative of liability under U.S.C. §1985[55] and, consequently, they themselves could be joined as defendants and prosecuted, they might be compelled to take appropriate action to terminate unlawful conspiratorial conduct.

---

55. *Grimes v. Smith*, 776 F.2d 1359 (D.C. Ind. 1985).

Chapter Eight

Civil RICO,
18 U.S.C. §§ 1961, 1962, 1964

Suing intelligence agency defendants, particularly CIA officers, under RICO—18 U.S.C. §§ 1961, 1962 and 1964—may be an innovative and effective method to confront certain conspiratorial, adverse personnel actions taken by agency officials. RICO's civil remedies subsection, 18 U.S.C. § 1964 (c), provides that "[A]ny person injured in his business or property by reason of a violation of section 1962" may sue in any appropriate district court and "shall recover threefold the damages he sustains and the cost of the suit, including a reasonable attorney's fee."

Eight elements must be pled for a plaintiff to avail himself or herself of the enhanced damage and attorney fees provision of civil RICO. They are:

(1) the defendant(s)
(2) through the commission of two of the enumerated predicate acts
(3) which constitute a pattern of
(4) racketeering activity
(5) directly or indirectly participate in the conduct of
(6) an enterprise,
(7) the activities of which affect interstate or foreign commerce, and
(8) plaintiff was injured in his business or property resulting from such conduct.[1]

The essence of civil RICO is the commission of two predicate acts in connection with the conduct of an enterprise.[2]

Subsections 18 U.S.C. § 1962 (c) and (d) on prohibited activities warrant particular emphasis in the context of the CIA. Subsection (c) states:

---

1. *Taylor v. Bear Stearns & Co.*, 572 F. Supp. 667 (D.C. Ga. 1983).
2. *Sedima v. Imrex Co.*, 473 U.S. 479 (1985).

It shall be unlawful for any *person employed by or associated with any enterprise* engaged in, or the *activities of which affect, interstate or foreign commerce*, to conduct or participate, directly or indirectly, in the conduct of such enterprise's affairs through a pattern of racketeering activity... (emphasis added).

Subsection (d) continues:

it shall be unlawful for any person to conspire to violate [the above subsection 18 U.S.C. § 1962 (c)].

The Supreme Court revolutionized private litigation in its broad interpretation of civil RICO in *Sedima v. Imrex Co.*[3] Although the *Sedima* decision has been criticized by some, it has not been overturned. The Court found justification for its holding in Congress' expansive language and overall approach, as well as in Congress' express admonition that RICO be liberally construed to effectuate its remedial purposes.[4]

The extensiveness and remedial purpose of RICO appear evident in the breadth of predicate offenses defined under 18 U.S.C. § 1961 (1). Among the many indictable racketeering activities which RICO encompasses, per 18 U.S.C. § 1961(1)(B), are those relating to: the obstruction of justice; the obstruction of criminal investigations; the obstruction of state or local law enforcement; tampering with a witness, victim or an informant; retaliating against a witness, victim, or an informant, and various kinds of fraud and misuse of documents.

Under 18 U.S.C. § 1961 (5), a "pattern of racketeering activity" requires at least two acts of racketeering activity. The Senate Report on this statute noted that the target of RICO is not sporadic, isolated activity; rather, continuity plus a relationship combine to produce a pattern.[5] In *H.J. Inc. v. Northwestern Bell Telephone Co.*, the Supreme Court again emphasized that a pattern of racketeering activity requires a relationship and continuity.[6] Alternatively, to establish a pattern, the plaintiff may show that the activity was a regular way of conducting the enterprise's ongoing business.[7] In its interpretation of a pattern of racketeering activity, the Supreme Court tried to send out a clear sig-

---

3. *Id.* at 497, 500.
4. *Id.* at 498.
5. S. Rep. No. 91-617, at 158 (1969).
6. *H.J. Inc. v. Northwestern Bell Tel. Co.*, 492 U.S. 229, 250 (1989).
7. *Id.*

nal that the RICO pattern element should not be ignored or treated in a perfunctory manner.[8]

Intelligence agency officials who take adverse personnel actions against another intelligence agency employee may be involved in a pattern of racketeering activity if, on at least two occasions, they obstruct justice by covering up, concealing or destroying evidence, fabricating, falsifying material facts, depriving another of equal protection of the law or taking reprisals against witnesses or victims in furtherance of any of these acts. CIA officers, because of their covert operational training and experience, may be more skilled in cover-up, concealment, reprisal, intimidation and clandestinity when engaging in such a pattern of activities than their organized crime counterparts and, therefore, accessing concealed evidence and fearful witnesses could be a monumental job.

In *Sedima*, the Supreme Court further held that predicate acts must involve conduct that is "indictable" or "chargeable."[9] Racketeering activity does not need to consist of acts for which the defendant has been convicted, only of acts for which he could be convicted. The Court pointed out that the plaintiff need not establish these predicate acts beyond a reasonable doubt.[10] Conduct that can be punished as criminal only upon proof beyond a reasonable doubt will support civil sanctions under a preponderance of evidence standard in civil RICO.[11]

Moreover in *Sedima*, the Court simplified the requirement to prove a civil RICO injury. It held that if the defendant engaged in a pattern of racketeering activities in a prohibited manner and these activities injured the plaintiff in his business or property, the plaintiff had a civil RICO claim.[12] The Court explained there was no room in the statutory language for the lower court's additional, amorphous "racketeering injury" requirement."[13]

"Enterprise," under 18 U.S.C. § 1961, likewise, is broadly defined and includes "any individual, partnership, corporation, association, or other legal entity, and any...group of individuals associated in fact although not a legal entity." In enacting this section of the statute Congress wanted to reach both

---

8. John E. Grenier & Sally S. Reilly, *Civil RICO—The Scope of Coverage After Sedima*, 47 Ala. Law. 260, 260-62 (1986) (discussing the RICO requirement of a pattern of racketeering activity).

9. *Sedima*, 473 U.S. at 488.

10. *Id.* at 490.

11. *Id.*

12. *Id.* at 495.

13. *Id.*

"legitimate" and "illegitimate" enterprises.[14] Legitimate enterprises "enjoy neither an inherent incapacity for criminal activity nor immunity from its consequences."[15] A *University of San Francisco Law Review* article, "Broadening the Scope of Civil RICO: Sedima S.P.R.L v. Imrex Co.," pointed out that RICO did not provide any exception for white-collar workers or business persons.[16] RICO was designed, instead, to provide a remedy for the use of racketeering practices in what would otherwise be considered legitimate businesses.[17] The court in *Haroco, Inc. v. American National Bank and Trust Co. of Chicago* explained that applying RICO to situations not expressly anticipated by Congress does not demonstrate ambiguity, it demonstrates breadth.[18]

Although the Supreme Court has yet to address the issue of whether RICO applies to government officials, at least eight circuit courts and one district court have found that a government entity constitutes an "enterprise" within the meaning of RICO.[19] In *United States v. Angelilli*, the court analyzed the language of RICO and concluded that the words "enterprise" and "include" indicate that the list is not exhaustive but merely illustrative, while "entity" denotes anything that exists.[20] The court in *United States v. Clark* used *Webster's New International Dictionary* and *Black's Law Dictionary* to define "enterprise" and decided that an enterprise could refer to any undertaking or systematic purposeful activity or to an entity with the capacity to function legally, sue or be sued and make decisions through agents.[21] In *United States v. Sisk*, the court also found that, given the simple, literal language of the statute, the definition of enterprise covered pub-

---

14. *United States v. Turkette*, 452 U.S. 576, 586-587 (1981).

15. *Sedima*, 473 U.S. at 499.

16. Faisal Shah, *Broadening the Scope of Civil RICO: Sedima S.P.R.L v. Imrex Co.*, 20 U.S.F. L. Rev. 339, 355 (1986).

17. *Id.*

18. *Haroco, Inc. v. Am. Nat'l Bank & Trust Co. of Chicago*, 747 F.2d 384, 398 (7th Cir. 1984.

19. *See, e.g., United States v. Freeman*, 6 F.3d 586, 596 (9th Cir. 1993); *United States v. Dozier*, 672 F.2d 531, 543 (5th Cir. 1982); *United States v. Thompson*, 685 F.2d 993, 998-1000 (6th Cir. 1982) (*en banc*); *United States v. Angelilli*, 660 F.2d 23, 30-35 (2d Cir. 1981); *United States v. Lee Stroller Enters.*, 652 F.2d 1313, 1313-19 (7th Cir. 1981); *United States v. Clark*, 646 F.2d 1259, 1261-67 (8th Cir. 1981); *United States v. Altomare*, 625 F.2d 5, 7 (4th Cir. 1980); *United States v. Bacheler*, 611 F.2d 443, 450 (3d Cir. 1979); *United States v. Sisk*, 476 F. Supp. 1061 (D. Tenn. 1979).

20. *United States v. Angelilli*, 660 F.2d 23, 31 (2d Cir. 1981).

21. *United States v. Clark*, 646 F.2d 1259, 1263 (8th Cir. 1981).

lic as well as private institutions and groups, including a governmental agency.[22] It seems clear from these decisions that a RICO enterprise may be found within a government agency.

The above cases all involved defendant government officials in positions such as staff aide to a legislator, marshal of a civil court, employee in a state governor's office and county judge, who were sued by the United States for various RICO-type conspiracies. The question, however, remains whether RICO similarly applies to federal officials. Given the courts' broad definitions of a RICO enterprise, which include a government entity or agency, and the broad construction of civil RICO since *Sedima*, there is a strong possibility that federal agencies, such as the CIA, and the activities of certain of their officers could be recognized as enterprises within the meaning of RICO.

Under 18 U.S.C. § 1962 (c), civil RICO also requires that the enterprise engage in activities which affect interstate or foreign commerce. The CIA, indeed, engages in activities that affect interstate and foreign commerce. Most of its activities cross United States borders and involve other countries, but the CIA also has offices throughout the United States. Moreover, to support its operations, the CIA involves itself in foreign and domestic commercial activities and, in the course of these operations, exploits the mail, telephone and computer systems and the internet.

It seems, therefore, that a CIA plaintiff may well have a cause of action under civil RICO against an enterprise consisting of CIA officers who conspire to commit two of the predicate acts enumerated under 18 U.S.C. § 1961 and whose activities affect interstate or foreign commerce. Such a claim, in fact, has already been brought against CIA officers by journalists in connection with a bombing during a Nicaraguan opposition leader's Costa Rican press conference.[23] This particular case was dismissed, not because the CIA was immune from RICO charges but because the journalists failed to present evidence that the defendants were responsible for their injuries.[24]

Since *Sedima*, civil RICO has been applied successfully in the courts to adverse personnel action-related cases. A *Nebraska Law Review* article, entitled "Employer's RICO Liability for the Wrongful Discharge of Their Employees," complained that RICO was upsetting the rules in labor and employment law.[25] The author noted that nowhere was this more evident than in the area of po-

---

22. *United States v. Sisk*, 476 F. Supp. 1061 (D. Tenn. 1979).

23. *Avirgan v. Hull*, 932 F.2d 1572 (11th Cir. 1991), *cert. denied*, 502 U.S. 1048 (1991).

24. *Id.*

25. Laura Ginger, *Employer's RICO Liability for the Wrongful Discharge of Their Employees*, 68 Neb. L. Rev. 673 (1989).

tential employer liability for employee discharges.[26] She also lamented that several districts courts have upheld the standing of former employees to employ a private civil RICO remedy against legitimate business entities.[27] Following *Sedima*, litigation under civil RICO in employee personnel-related matters indeed has been liberalized to the benefit of the aggrieved employee.

For example, in *Acampora v. Boise Cascade Corp.*, the court found that under the liberal standing requirements outlined in *Sedima*, a discharged employee had standing to bring a civil RICO action for allegations that the defendant was engaged in a pattern of racketeering activity, that plaintiff discovered the illegal activity and that, as a result, the defendant harassed her and eventually caused her to lose her job.[28] The court noted that the injury alleged by the plaintiff—the loss of job—flowed from the defendant's commission of a pattern of racketeering activity and a cover-up of those predicate acts in connection with the conduct of an enterprise.[29] The court was persuaded that the alleged injury was sufficiently related to the defendant's illegal conduct to maintain the action.[30] It also pointed out that the racketeering activity could personally benefit the defendant and need not benefit the enterprise in order to come within RICO's ambit.[31] Lastly, the *Acampora* court decided that the plaintiff had sufficiently alleged that the defendant utilized his position within the enterprise to engage in racketeering activity and thus stated a claim under RICO.[32]

Civil RICO's trebled damage element in employment-related cases means that awards may be substantial. For example, a federal jury awarded two former executives of a petroleum company nearly 70 million dollars after finding that the company's top executives had wrongfully discharged them for protesting alleged illegal foreign payments.[33] The plaintiffs claimed violations of 18 U.S.C. § 1962 (a), (c), and (d), and both indirect and/or direct injuries.[34] As part of the conspiracy to violate RICO, they argued that the conspirators eliminated their opposition within the company to cover-up illegalities. The plaintiffs said they were discharged and discredited as part of the cover-up. These actions constituted overt acts in furtherance of the conspiracy, even

---

26. *Id.*

27. *Id.* at 675.

28. *Acampora v. Boise Cascade Corp.*, 635 F. Supp. 66, 69 (D.N.J. 1986).

29. *Id.*

30. *Id.*

31. *Id.*

32. *Id.* at 70.

33. Sharon E. Epperson, *Jury Awards 2 Ashland Oil Ex-Officials $70 Million in Suit Over Their Dismissal*, Wall St. J., June 14, 1988, at 5.

34. *Williams v. Hall*, 683 F. Supp. 639, 641 (E.D. Ky. 1988).

though they might not have been prohibited predicate acts.[35] The court held that the plaintiffs had standing to sue under RICO for their discharge and resulting damages if they could prove that the terminations were overt acts done in furtherance of a conspiracy to operate the company through a pattern of racketeering activity, even though their only injuries were caused by overt, not predicate, acts.[36] In justifying its decision, the court looked to *Sedima* and decided *Sedima* dictated a liberal construction of RICO. It found damage from a RICO conspiracy was actionable to the same extent as damage from a common law or antitrust conspiracy, and a plaintiff who had proven a 18 U.S.C. § 1962 (d) conspiracy to violate 18 U.S.C. § 1962 (a) or (c) had standing to recover threefold, upon showing injury from any overt acts done pursuant to the conspiracy.[37]

In another adverse personal-related civil RICO action, the court discussed indirect and direct civil RICO injuries.[38] It noted that some forums have ruled that a whistleblower discharge is only indirectly caused by the pattern of illegal conduct alleged and, therefore, not susceptible to RICO relief.[39] Nevertheless, it decided that since the Eighth Circuit seemed to be holding firm in allowing RICO recoveries when illegal conduct indirectly harmed the plaintiff, the plaintiff, who had been indirectly harmed as a result of a scheme involving a cover-up, could have leave to amend his complaint.[40]

On the other hand, the plaintiff in *Reddy v. Litton Industries, Inc.* charged his employer with RICO violations and alleged he was wrongfully discharged from his job because he refused to participate in the employer's illegal cover-up.[41] While acknowledging that other courts have held acts in furtherance of a conspiracy may be RICO violations under 18 U.S.C. § 1962 (d), in *Reddy*, the court decided against the plaintiff on the grounds that the injury suffered was caused by the wrongful discharge, which was not a predicate act under 18 U.S.C. § 1961 (1).[42] This decision has since been criticized by the third, seventh and eighth circuit courts.

The bottom line appears to be that, given the expansive construction of civil RICO in recent years and the broad definition of "enterprise" accorded by the

---

35. *Id.* at 642.
36. *Id.*
37. *Id.* at 643.
38. *Komm v. McFliker*, 662 F. Supp. 924, 926 (W.D. Mo. 1987).
39. *Id.* at 927.
40. *Id.* at 928.
41. *Reddy v. Litton Indus. Inc.*, 912 F.2d 291, 294 (9th Cir. 1990).
42. *Id.*

courts, the conspiratorial activities of certain intelligence agency officers in some areas, to include those related to adverse personnel actions, may well come within the reach of a civil RICO suit. Certainly the CIA's past conduct has shown that its personnel may have committed racketeering activity, as defined in 18 U.S.C. § 1961, involving two predicate acts in connection with the conduct of an enterprise whose activities affect interstate or foreign commerce.

CHAPTER NINE

ADMINISTRATIVE AND PROCEDURAL REMEDIES

The plaintiff pursuing a legal action against U.S. Intelligence is faced with a variety of problems unique to suing an intelligence agency, many related to the misuse of security to control evidence and witnesses. To deal with the serious inequities, administrative and procedural remedies do exist and are already being used in non-intelligence agency civil action contexts. Certain methods and rules could and should be enforced with rigor vis-a-vis intelligence agencies, particularly the CIA, in an effort to level the playing field and confront some of the worst injustices.

This Chapter suggests and discusses a variety of possible administrative and procedural solutions to problems relative to civil actions against U.S. Intelligence. Pursuant to the Federal Rules of Civil Procedure, for example, the intelligence agencies should be obliged to enter into mandatory, early and cooperative discovery to supplement and correct its disclosures and responses and to undergo sanctions for non-compliance and obstruction. The issue of confidentiality has been handled and resolved by the courts in a variety of ways including: in camera judicial review; using a court-appointed master to determine what classified documents can be given to opposing counsel; a statement admitting the relevant facts which the classified information would tend to prove, and the substitution for the classified information of a summary which would provide plaintiffs with substantially the same ability to make their case as would disclosure. Additionally, if a recalcitrant intelligence agency is still unwilling to comply with discovery, the burden of proof could be shifted to the agency and the standard of proof could be elevated from the preponderance of evidence to clear and convincing. Other government agencies which grant security clearances should be used instead of the CIA to provide the clearances on CIA plaintiffs' counselors. CIA employees also would benefit by their inclusion in the protections offered to civil service whistle-blowers under the Whistleblowers Protection Act of 1989.[1]

Remedying the situation calls for judicial and legislative activism. The solutions are not necessarily new and untried. What would probably work best in dealing with the CIA's abuse of secrecy would be to combine and exploit a variety of administrative and procedural remedies which are potentially available against this bureaucratic Goliath.

A. Requiring Compliance with Federal Rules of Civil Procedure (FRCP)

Obstructionary tactics by intelligence agencies create numerous unfair difficulties and obstacles for litigants who are apt to be already stressed emotionally and financially from adverse personnel actions taken against them and their attempts to redress these wrongs. These tactics include, but are not limited to, impeding and preventing discovery under the guise of secrecy and national security through the agencies' complete control over evidence and potential witnesses and through the invocation of the state secrets privilege.

1. FRCP—Rule 26. General Provisions Governing Discovery; Duty of Disclosure

a. Required Disclosure; Methods to Discover Additional Matters

The harm to the plaintiff caused by an intelligence agency's control of evidence and personnel and its obstruction of and non-compliance with discovery could be rectified at least to some extent if all federal courts required all federal agencies to abide by the existing Federal Rules of Civil Procedure, specifically Rule 26(a)—"General Provisions Governing Discovery; Duty of Disclosure," "Required Disclosure and Methods to Discover Additional Matters." This section codifies a positive trend toward encouraging both sides to cooperate without delay in the interest of justice in an effort to uncover and reveal relevant evidence, facilitating the early exchange of pertinent information between

---

1. Whistleblower Protection Act of 1989 (WPA), Pub. L. No. 101-12, § 3(i), 103 Stat. 16; 5 U.S.C. § 1201 (West 1996).

parties. Particularly important to enforce upon the intelligence agencies would be the Rule 26(a)(1) requirement concerning *Initial Disclosures:*

> a party must, without awaiting a discovery request, provide to other parties:
>> (A) the name and, if known, the address and telephone number of each individual likely to have discoverable information that the disclosing party may use to support its claims or defenses...identifying the subjects of the information;
>> (B) a copy of, or a description by category and location of, all documents, data compilations, and tangible things that are in the possession, custody, or control of the party and that the disclosing party may use to support its claims or defenses....
> A party must make its initial disclosures based on information then reasonably available to it and is not excused from making its disclosures because it has not fully completed its investigation of the case or because it challenges the sufficiency of another party's disclosures or because another party has not made its disclosures.[2]

In litigating against a U.S. intelligence agency for alleged unlawful adverse personnel actions, this automatic exchange of information would indeed help advance and focus the action, identify relevant evidence and narrow the issues. Early mandatory discovery and disclosure, in fact, could bring about the settlement or termination of a dispute well before trial.

Since the pleading is supposed to contain only a short and plain statement of the claims showing the plaintiff is entitled to relief, an intelligence agency might try to circumvent Rule 26(a) by arguing that the allegations are too broad to provide sufficient notice. To preclude this possibility, required discovery could apply in a suit against U.S. intellgience agencies to Complaints, whether alleged with particularity or averred more generally.

b. Supplementation of Disclosures and Responses; Conference of Parties; Planning for Discovery

Rules 26(e) "Supplementation of Disclosures and Responses" and 26(f) "Conference of Parties; Planning for Discovery" are two additional procedural rules concerning discovery to which the federal courts should require intelligence agencies to adhere scrupulously. These Rules similarly encourage cooperation and expedition rather than obstruction.

---

2. Fed. R. Civ. P. 26(a)(1).

Under the 26(e), intelligence agencies would be duty bound to supplement and amend discovery to include disclosing newly acquired information. Specifically,

> A party who has made disclosure under subdivision (a) or responded to a request for discovery with a disclosure or response is under a duty to supplement or correct the disclosure or response to include information thereafter acquired…in the following circumstances:
>
> 1) A party is under a duty to supplement at appropriate intervals its disclosures…if the party learns that in some material respect the information disclosed is incomplete or incorrect and if the additional or corrective information has not otherwise been made known to the other parties during the discovery process or in writing.…
>
> (2) A party is under a duty seasonably to amend a prior response to an interrogatory, request for production, or request for admission if the party learns that the response is in some material respect incomplete or incorrect and if the additional corrective information has not otherwise been made known to the other parties during the discovery process or in writing.[3]

In addition, Rule 26(f) requires the parties to confer to, among other things, consider the possibilities for a prompt settlement or resolution of the case and make or arrange for the required disclosures, as well as to develop a proposed discovery plan.[4] The attorneys are jointly responsible "for attempting in good faith to agree on the proposed discovery plan, and for submitting to the court within 14 days after the conference a written report outlining the plan."[5]

Rule 26 can be superseded by local court rules, but allowing trial courts to control discovery raises questions regarding uniformity. Variations would not be a problem if, at a minimum, the rules of the local courts were as strong and progressive as the Federal Rules of Civil Procedures. When litigation is against an intelligence agency, the courts should be consistent in holding the defendant and the plaintiff to the standards established by the revised Federal Rules of Civil Procedure or local courts, whichever is higher.

---

3. Fed. R. Civ. P. 26(e).
4. Fed. R. Civ. P. 26(f).
5. *Id.*

2. FRCP—Rule 37. Failure to Make or Cooperate in Discovery: Sanctions

To ensure that an intelligence agency does not find a way to delay, obstruct or evade proper discovery, Rule 37—"Failure to Make or Cooperate in Discovery: Sanctions"—should be fairly but, as necessary, strictly enforced, particularly against the CIA. Non-compliance with discovery could include the failure to honestly and fully provide mandatory disclosures, to answer questions in interrogatories and admissions, to permit inspection or to attend ones own deposition.[6] The provision of false, misleading, evasive or incomplete disclosure or responses likewise should be treated as failure to make or cooperate in discovery.[7]

Rule 37 furnishes a range of serious sanctions depending on the violation, the intent, reasons, circumstances and consequences.[8] For example, if a motion to compel discovery or disclosure is disobeyed or the party or a party's attorney fails to participate in good faith in the development of a discovery plan, the court may require the party or attorney or both to pay the opposing counsel's fees and expenses caused by the failure.[9] The court also may order that certain facts against a disobeying party are taken as established for the purpose of the action.[10] Another sanction could preclude a party from supporting or opposing designated claims or defenses or from introducing these matters into evidence.[11] In addition, the court could order the striking of pleadings or parts thereof or treating the failure to comply as contempt of court.[12]

Rendering a judgment by default against the disobedient party is yet another option which courts may choose.[13] A penalty default is appropriate under certain circumstances. Most frequently it is used in cases where the defendant willfully refuses to comply with a court order for pretrial discovery.[14]

---

6. Fed. R. Civ. P. 37.

7. Fed. R. Civ. P. 37 (a)(3).

8. Fed. R. Civ. P. 37 (a)(4)(A), 37(b)(2), 37(c), 37(g).

9. Fed. R. Civ. P. 37 (a)(4), 37(b)(2), 37(g).

10. Fed. R. Civ. P. 37 (b)(2)(A).

11. Fed. R. Civ. P. 37 (b)(2)(B).

12. Fed. R. Civ. P. 37 (b)(2)(C), (D).

13. *See Vitale v. Elliott*, 387 A.2d. 1379, 1382 (R.I. 1978) (reaffirming default judgment), *and* Fed. R. Civ. P. 37 (b)(2)(C).

14. *Trans World Airlines, Inc. v. Hughes*, 449 F.2d 51, 58, 60 (2d Cir. 1965) (defendant refused to comply with discovery).

If intelligence agency officials knew that the federal courts would not hesitate to impose sanctions for abusing the discovery process, they would no doubt exploit their skills and ingenuity to find ways to facilitate the exchange of information, as the Federal Rules of Civil Procedure intended. Mandatory cooperation and honesty would serve justice, as well as assist already beleaguered plaintiffs.

B. Other Procedural Suggestions for Handling Problems Associated with U.S. Intelligence

In addition to problems related to discovery, plaintiffs suing intelligence agencies always are faced with its claims of secrecy and national security. Sometimes, real issues of security may be involved. Other times, intelligence agencies such as the CIA overclassify or redact information or claim the state secrets privilege merely because the evidence is unfavorable or embarrassing. With the possible exception of documentation requested under the Freedom of Information Act, the courts likely will not consider challenges to issues of classification or redaction.[15] They generally adhere to the policy that the determination of whether to designate information as classified is a matter committed to the Executive Branch.[16]

Nonetheless, there are workable ways to overcome the problems where confidential information may be material to litigation. They include: in camera judicial review; appointing a master; the substitution for classified information of a summary sufficient to provide plaintiffs with the same ability to make their case as disclosure, and a stipulation or statement whereby the intelligence agency would admit the relevant facts which the classified information would tend to prove.

1. In Camera Judicial Review

Legal precedent clearly exists for in camera review. The Supreme Court, in fact, has commended in camera judicial review of documents in discovery to ensure striking a proper balance between confidentiality and disclosure.[17] In *Kerr v. United States District Court*, a dispute arose regarding the discovery of

---

15. *United States v. Musa*, 833 F. Supp. 752, 755 (E.D. Mo. 1993).
16. *Id.*
17. *Kerr v. United States Dist. Court*, 96 S. Ct. 2119, 2125 (1976).

California Adult Authority documentation, including personnel files and a sample of prisoner files. The Court noted that the trial judge had an appropriate avenue—in camera review of materials—to achieve precisely the relief sought.[18] The Court described this procedure as a "relatively costless and eminently worthwhile method" to balance the claims of irrelevance and confidentiality with the assertion of necessity.[19]

In camera review also has been used in discrimination cases to preclude the potential abuse of the redaction process and facilitate discovery. In *EEOC v. University of Notre Dame Du Lac*, for example, the court ordered the files on faculty tenure deliberations redacted to remove any information that might identify deliberating faculty members.[20] The redactions then would be reviewed in camera by the district court judge, who would have the originals before him for comparison. Counsel for both parties would be present and able to read the redacted files. If the files turned out to contain evidence or leads to evidence of discrimination, the plaintiff's attorney could request the judge to order the names revealed so that relevant persons could be deposed.[21]

In an antitrust case, *Marrese v. American Academy of Orthopaedic Surgeons*, Judge Richard Posner pointed out that barring the plaintiffs or their counsel from access to membership files probably would make it impossible for them to prove their case.[22] Clearly such a barrier would not serve justice. Judge Posner recognized that there were various devices available to the district judge to reconcile parties' competing needs. Acknowledging that the files might be voluminous, nonetheless, the judge recommended in camera examination for evidence of any anticompetitive purpose, beginning with the files of the plaintiffs.[23]

The time and effort of in camera review may be the cost of justice. For intelligence agency employees litigating against their employer, it could mean their professional survival and livelihood.

2. Appointment of Master

There is also legal precedent for appointing a special master who has been granted a security clearance to decide what classified documents can be pro-

---

18. *Id.*
19. *Id.*
20. *EEOC v. Univ. of Notre Dame Du Lac*, 715 F.2d 331, 338-39 (7th Cir. 1983).
21. *Id.*
22. *Marrese v. Am. Acad. of Orthopaedic Surgeons*, 726 F.2d 1150, 1160 (7th Cir. 1984).
23. *Id.*

vided to the attorneys for a plaintiff suing the federal government. It is the court itself that determines that a master is needed and makes the appointment. According to an Associated Press release, dated June 1, 2001, United States District Court Judge for the District of Columbia, Thomas Penfield Jackson, was faced with the dilemma of how to handle sensitive information requested by the lawyers of former nuclear scientist, Wen Ho-lee, in a defamation suit.[24] Judge Jackson decided to appoint a special master to supervise the handling and dissemination of classified documents to Lee's attorneys.

3. Providing Summary of Classified Information Sufficient to Substitute for Disclosure; Admission of Relevant Facts; Finding against U.S. Intelligence; Striking Testimony of Witness

Additional alternative procedures related to the disclosure of relevant classified information are incorporated into the Classified Information Procedures Act (CIPA), which itself now is applicable only in criminal cases.[25] Many of these procedures could be employed analogically in civil actions against U.S. intelligence agencies to handle problems of discovery including overclassification and redaction. There is, after all, an identity of interest in fairness and justice no matter whether the litigation is civil or criminal.

CIPA was designed to establish procedures to harmonize the defendant's right to obtain and present exculpatory material and the government's right to protect classified information by requiring rulings on admissibility of classified information before trial.[26] The purpose of CIPA, and the aim of this Chapter on administrative and procedural remedies, is similar—to find a balance in light of the government's control over information and witnesses. Some of the procedures laid out in CIPA, therefore, could lend themselves well to civil actions against an intelligence agency.

Regarding relevancy of evidence, CIPA states that the "[d]istrict court may not take into account that evidence is classified when determining its use, relevancy, or admissibility."[27] Relevance, even of classified information, is gov-

---

24. Robert Gehrke, *Judge to Appoint Master in Lee Case*, Associated Press, June 1, 2001, *available at* http://www.lanl.gov.

25. Classified Information Procedures Act, 18 U.S.C.A. app. 3 (West 2000).

26. *United States v. Pappas*, 94 F.3d 795, 799 (2d Cir. 1996).

27. *See supra* note 25 at 18 USC App. §§3, 6(f)(2).

erned solely by the standards established in the Federal Rules of Evidence.[28] This criteria would apply in cases involving U.S. intelligence agencies whether the action is civil or criminal.

CIPA allows for the court, upon request, to make determinations concerning the disclosure of specific classified information. If the court authorizes the disclosure:

> [T]he United States may move that, in lieu of this disclosure of such specific classified information, the court order:
> (A) the substitution for such classified information of a statement admitting relevant facts that the specific classified information would tend to prove; or
> (B) the substitution for such classified information of a summary of the specific classified information.
> The court shall grant such a motion if it finds that the statement or summary will provide the defendant with substantially the same ability to make his defense as would disclosure of the specific classified information.[29]

CIPA also suggests other remedies for the defendant when the United States impedes discovery. Relief may include, but is not limited to, a finding against the government on any issue to which the excluded classified information relates or the striking or precluding of all or part of the related testimony of a government witness.[30]

CIPA provides some fertile ground to find equitable administrative and procedural methods for handling an intelligence agency's refusal to disclose information. Solutions may include allowing the agency to substitute a summary of information for classified documentation if the substitution or admission would provide the plaintiff with substantially the same ability to make his or her case as would disclosure or requiring a stipulation to or admission of the relevant facts that the classified information would tend to prove. Other ways to handle an agency's refusal to cooperate with discovery would be for the court to strike the testimony of an agency witness or find against the intelligence agency on any issue to which the excluded classified information relates. By using a combination of these methods, judges may begin to bring some equity and balance to the proceedings.

---

28. *Id.*
29. 18 U.S.C.A. app. 3, §6(c)(1) (West 2000).
30. *Id.* at §§6(e)(1), 6(e)(2)(b), and (e)(2)(C).

C. Shifting Burden of Proof to Defendant-U.S. Intelligence Agency

A more innovative, but workable and recognized, approach to solving the problem where one party controls the information and potential witnesses and exploits secrecy to prevent necessary discovery is to shift the burden of proof. Specifically, the defendant intelligence agency, rather than the plaintiff, could and probably should have the burden of persuasion at trial. This change would assist in rectifying some of the gross disadvantages suffered by plaintiffs who try to sue a U.S. intelligence agency.

Shifting the burden is related to the well-established doctrine of *res ipsa loquitur*, a rule of evidence whereby the defendant's negligence may be inferred from the character of an accident, but the instrumentality that caused the injury is under the management and exclusive control of the defendant. In such situations, the defendant needs to produce the evidence to rebut this presumption. Wigmore noted that "the particular force and justice of the rule... consists in the circumstance that the chief evidence of the true cause... is practically accessible to [the defendant] but inaccessible to the injured person."[31]

An analogue to situations where the doctrine of *res ipsa loquitur* is applied is the "conspiracy of silence" among physicians, medical personnel and the hospital which control the information regarding a patient's unexplained injury that occurred while he or she was unconscious during an operation. In such situations "one may suspect the courts... [would not be] reluctant to even the balance against the professional conspiracy of silence."[32] A similar need for equity and common sense may be called for when suing U.S. Intelligence.

The doctrine of *res ipsa loquitur*, in fact, has been expanded and applied to other situations. The New Jersey Supreme Court, for example, has broadened this rule of evidence to embrace cases where there are alternate theories of liability and multiple defendants who control the instrumentalities and the information.[33] In such cases, the defendants are required to come forward and present their evidence. This concept has been called "akin to *res ipsa loquitur*" or "conditional *res ipsa loquitur*."[34]

Still other legal precedent exists for shifting the burden of proof. When a plaintiff was accidentally shot by a hunter, for instance, and there were two

---

31. 9 J. Wigmore, *Treatise on Evidence* 382, § 2509 (3d ed. 1940).
32. William Prosser, *Selected Topics on the Law of Torts*, 346 (1954).
33. *Anderson v. Somberg*, 67 N.J. 291, 298-300, 306-08 (1975).
34. *Id.*

hunters, both negligently shooting, the court determined that it would be unjust to require the plaintiff to pin the injury on one wrongdoer.[35] The requirement to shift the burden of proof to the defendants in such a situation became manifest.[36]

In another suit, where 13 infant plaintiffs were all injured in separate blasting cap accidents, the six corporate defendants argued that the plaintiff should not be allowed to shift the burden of proof on causation because the caps could have been made by parties not named as defendants.[37] The court, nevertheless, held that if the plaintiffs could establish it was more likely than not that one of the defendants manufactured the particular cap that caused the injury, then the burden was on each defendant to show that its caps were not involved in that particular accident.[38]

In yet another case, a plaintiff was injured as a result of a drug administered to her mother during pregnancy.[39] She knew the type of drug but could not identify the manufacturer of the precise product. The plaintiff relied on cases in which a party could not identify which of two or more defendants caused an injury and, therefore, the burden of proof shifted to the defendants to show they were not responsible. Here the court held each defendant liable for the proportion of the judgment represented by its share of the market, unless the defendant could demonstrate that it could not have made the product that caused the plaintiff's injury.[40]

The principle here, sometimes referred to as the "alternate liability" theory, is embodied in the Restatements of Torts:

> Where the conduct of two or more actors is tortious, and it is proved that harm has been caused to the plaintiff by only one of them, but there is uncertainty as to which one has caused it, the burden is upon each such actor to prove that he has not caused the harm.[41]
>
> [The underlying reason for the Rule is] the injustice of permitting proved wrongdoers, who among them have inflicted an injury...to escape liability merely because the nature of their conduct and the re-

---

35. *Summers v. Tice*, 33 Cal. 2d 80, 81 (1948).
36. *Id.*
37. *Hall v. E.I. du Pont de Nemours & Co.*, 345 F. Supp. 353, 378-80 (E.D.N.Y. 1972).
38. *Id.*
39. *Sindell v. Abbot Labs.*, 607 P.2d 924 (Cal. 1980).
40. *Id.* at 937.
41. Restatement (Second) of Torts § 433B(3) (1965).

sulting harm has made it difficult or impossible to prove which of them has caused the harm.[42]

Shifting the burden, in fact, has been legislated specifically for certain discrimination cases in the Civil Rights Act of 1964. In a reverse discrimination suit, for example, the first burden is on the employer to produce evidence that its affirmative action program was a response to a conspicuous racial imbalance in its work force and is remedial.[43] The second burden is also on the employer to produce evidence that its affirmative action plan is reasonably related to the plan's remedial purpose.[44] It is only after the employer meets its first and second burdens that the employee needs to present evidence to show that some reason other than a remedial reason motivated the employer or that the adopted plan unreasonably exceeded its remedial purpose.[45] Since the initial burdens of production are on the employer, pleading requirements in a reverse discrimination case are more rigorous.[46]

Although an affirmative action plan which is discriminatory on its face is distinguishable from a case involving an employee suing an intelligence agency, it demonstrates that in certain circumstances Congress is able to and has legislated burden shifting in employment actions. Where, for instance, a recalcitrant and powerful CIA controls all information and witnesses, it may be similarly appropriate for Congress to legislate shifting the burden of proof.

D. Changing Standard of Proof to Clear and Convincing

Another suggestion aimed at bringing some balance and equity into litigation between a solitary plaintiff and an intelligence agency after the burden of proof is shifted to the government would be to require the agency and its officials to meet the higher clear and convincing standard rather than the easier preponderance of evidence standard. There is precedent for requiring a heightened burden of proof from the government. Specifically under the amended Whistleblower Protection Act of 1989 (WPA), the alleged wrongdoer agency must prove its defense by the legally more stringent clear and con-

---

42. Restatement (Second) of Torts § 433B cmt. f (1965).
43. Title VII of the Civil Rights Act of 1964, as amended Pub. L. No. 102-166 (1991).
44. *Id.*
45. *Id.*
46. *Stroud v. Seminole Tribe of Fla.*, 574 F. Supp. 1043, 1044 (S.D. Fla. 1983).

vincing evidence standard.[47] Essentially, Congress wanted to send a strong, clear signal that reprisals against whistleblowers would not be tolerated. The legislative intent of the amendment to the Act was laid out in the following joint explanatory statement to Congress:

> "Clear and convincing evidence" is a high burden of proof for the Government....This heightened burden of proof...recognizes that when it comes to proving the basis for an agency's decision, the agency controls most of the cards—the drafting of the documents supporting the decision, the testimony of witnesses who participated in the decision, and the records that could document whether similar personnel actions have been taken in other cases. In these circumstances, it is entirely appropriate that the agency bear a heavy burden to justify its actions.[48]

These words are directly applicable in employment-related law suits against an intelligence agency where the agency controls all the cards—the documents, the witnesses and the historical records. It is entirely appropriate, therefore, that the intelligence agency bear a heavy burden to justify its actions.

The amended WPA contains yet another important provision that could be applied in litigation against an intelligence agency, particularly the CIA, which would make it easier for an individual to prove reprisal and retaliation. The complainant now needs only show that the whistleblowing was a "contributing factor" in an agency decision to take an adverse personnel action against him or her.[49] This amendment supersedes the requirement that whistleblowing be a "significant factor" in the retaliation.[50]

The then Attorney General Richard Thornburgh sent a letter to Senator Carl Levin, dated March 3, 1989, expressing support for the changes. He explained:

> a "contributing factor" need not be "substantial." The individual's burden is to prove that the whistleblowing contributed in some way to the agency's decision to take the (adverse) personnel action.[51]

The joint explanatory statement to Congress also pointed out that there are many ways to establish that whistleblowing was a factor in the adverse per-

---

47. *See supra* note 1.
48. 135 Cong. Rec. H749 (daily ed. Mar. 21, 1989) (Joint Explanatory Statement on S. 508,7. Burden of Proof).
49. *Id.*
50. *Id.*
51. *Id.*

sonnel action. The statement suggested that one can show the official taking the action knew or had constructive knowledge of the disclosure if the official acted within such a period of time that a reasonable person could conclude that the disclosure was a factor in the personnel action.[52]

E. Security Clearances for Opposing Counsel

One of the very first items on the agenda of a complainant contemplating a law suit is hiring a lawyer. A CIA employee's choice of counsel, however, is controlled and hindered by the CIA from the very beginning of the legal process. The CIA insists that CIA employees, or even CIA spouses in potential litigation against the Agency or its officials, first obtain a CIA security clearance on their would-be lawyer before retaining him or her (see Chapter One, Section A).

The standards and procedures governing the granting of United States government security clearances are set forth in a variety of legislative statutes and executive orders and in a Director of Central Intelligence Directive.[53] Nowhere does it appear in the law that the CIA and only the CIA has the power and authority to provide security clearances to lawyers suing the CIA or Agency employees. Nevertheless, the CIA tries to impose this requirement and to wield the power to decide which lawyers will and will not be allowed to sue the Agency. This phenomena is quite amazing—it gives the defendant the power to control the selection and number of its opponents in the adversarial process!

Allowing the CIA to decide which attorneys will litigate against the Agency may have serious due process implications. The right to counsel is guaranteed by the Sixth Amendment to the Constitution in all criminal cases. The due process clause of the Fifth Amendment could be interpreted to extend this right to employee-litigants in civil actions where liberty or property interests are implicated. The Fifth Circuit has even found a right to counsel in civil cases

---

52. *Id.*

53. Director of Central Intelligence Directive 1/14 (Apr. 14, 1986); Intelligence Identities Protection Act of 1982; Subversive Activities Act of 1950, § 4(b); National Security Act of 1947, § 103(c)(5); 50 U.S.C. § 403-3; 50 U.S.C. § 421; 50 U.S.C. § 783(b); 18 U.S.C. §§ 641, 793, 794, 798; Exec. Order No. 12,333; Exec. Order No. 12,356, 46 Fed. Reg. 59, 941, 1081.

independent of a protected liberty or property interest.[54] In addition, the Equal Employment Opportunity Commission's Management Directive—110 permits the aggrieved party in an employment discrimination suit to be represented at every stage of the process. Although there does not appear to be settled law on a due process right to a lawyer of one's choice, generally any American, other than a CIA employee, may retain the legal representative he or she selects.

Specific problems for litigants and their counsel created by the CIA's control of the security clearance process and security for opposing counsel are, inter alia:

(1) the CIA has the power to grant or withhold the security clearance on any prospective lawyer whom an employee plans to retain;

(2) using this power, the CIA exerts control over the legal process and opposing counsel from the very inception of a case;

(3) by controlling the clearance process, the CIA decides which lawyers and law firm personnel work against it;

(4) by controlling the clearance process, the CIA decides how many lawyers may work against it and generally limits the number to one attorney, no matter how complicated the case and how many attorneys the CIA and the Department of Justice (DOJ) have working on the case;

(5) an attorney who receives a CIA security clearance for one case is not cleared to work on another CIA case;

(6) the CIA security clearance process for opposing counsel may be prolonged up to six weeks and can result in an employee losing an opportunity to file a timely complaint while awaiting the clearance (if the CIA so chooses, it can clear a lawyer in less than 24 hours);

(7) a CIA employee working under cover is not allowed to discuss any work-related matter, to include his or her name, with an uncleared attorney;

(8) an attorney who is granted a CIA clearance is required to sign a secrecy agreement with the CIA as a prerequisite to representing a CIA client. The secrecy agreement works to intimidate attorneys, limit their First Amendment rights, and place them and their client's case under the CIA's control;

---

54. *See McCuin v. Tex. Power & Light Co.*, 714 F.2d 1255, 1262 & n.24 (5th Cir. 1983) and *Tex. Catastrophe Prop. Ins. Ass'n v. Morales*, 975 F.2d 1178, 1181 (5th Cir. 1992), *cert. denied* 507 U.S. 1018 (1993).

(9) even non-CIA employees and their lawyers, such as wives involved in divorce proceedings against their CIA spouses, are forced to sign CIA secrecy agreements (see Chapter One, Section A.3);

(10) despite having a CIA security clearance and signing a secrecy agreement, opposing counsel generally is not allowed to see classified or unclassified information needed for litigation purposes, including CIA regulations, rules and policies, the client's personnel, medical and security files or the results of an investigation of the client, including one conducted by the Office of the Inspector General;

(11) a CIA employee generally is not supposed to discuss classified matters with his or her Agency-cleared attorney;

(12) the CIA attempts to force opposing counsel to work at CIA headquarters and use only Agency computers in its litigation work against the CIA, giving the Agency the ability to access privileged attorney-client information;

(13) the CIA gains access to privileged attorney-client information by screening all information in advance of allowing clients to show any material to an attorney and checking lawyers' notes before counsel can leave a CIA facility;

(14) the CIA also acquires access to attorney-client information through its control of the redaction process, and

(15) a conflict of interest develops if the CIA selectively grants security clearances to certain lawyers to represent employees suing the CIA. These attorneys "owe" some of their clients to the CIA and have an interest in maintaining good relations with the CIA in order to remain on the Agency's cleared lawyer list.

The myriad of problems cited above can be rectified to a large extent by removing the security clearance process for opposing attorneys from CIA control. Since various other government agencies, particularly the Department of Justice in conjunction with the Federal Bureau of Investigation and the Department of Defense, have more than adequate security standards and procedures in place, their offices can and should be used to provide the necessary clearances for lawyers representing CIA clients.

A clearance from a competent non-CIA federal government agency should be granted in a timely manner to a prospective attorney representing a plaintiff suing the CIA unless good cause can be shown for withholding a clearance. An attorney who is refused a clearance should be notified in writing why the clearance is being withheld. "Good cause" should not be that the attorney prevailed in another suit against the CIA or against a United States government agency. Once cleared, an attorney should be able to work on any case against the CIA or another intelligence agency at least during the period of time the clearance remains valid and in force. In addition, it must be the client's and his or her counsel's decision, not the defendant-intelligence agency's, how many cleared lawyers and legal personnel are needed to work on the case. Just as plaintiffs would never be allowed to determine who and how many attorneys from the CIA's legal staff or the DOJ may oppose them, the CIA should not be able to dictate such matters to plaintiffs.

Moreover, cleared attorneys must be allowed to see the information they need to pursue a case, whether or not the documents are classified. If no classified information is involved and the employee is overt, no clearance should be required. The CIA should not be able to impose its security regulations and clearance process on non-Agency employees just because they are married to CIA persons. Lastly, lawyers must not surrender to CIA attempts to force them to work at CIA headquarters, use CIA computers in preparing for litigation against the CIA and select and screen the information they need to see and the notes they take. In addition to being seriously inconvenient and costly, such procedures give the CIA access to its opponent's privileged attorney-client information and confidential work product.

F. Extend Benefits of Whistleblower Protection Act to CIA Employees

As noted above, the CIA is exempt from the 1989 Whistleblower Protection Act (WPA).[55] The WPA does not extend to "any Executive Agency or unit thereof, the principal function of which is the conduct of foreign intelligence or counterintelligence activities."[56] In keeping with its hands-off policy toward government employees who work in intelligence, the Office of Special Counsel, established under the WPA, does not appear to have any provisions for handling classified material or for authorizing disclosure of such information, if necessary.[57] This void has denied CIA employees the right to protection from retribution which other United States government employees

---

55. *See supra* note 1.

56. 5 U.S.C.A. §2302(a)(2)(C)(i) (West 1996).

57. Bruce D. Fisher, *Whistleblower Protection Act—A False Hope for Whistleblowers*, 43 Rutgers L. Rev. 355, 400-16 (1991) (pointing to serious problems in implementation of objectives of the Whistleblower Protection Act such as turning over investigation and writing of reports responding to whistleblower's allegations to agency on which whistle was

enjoy. It has allowed the CIA to take reprisals at will against those who report Agency wrongdoing.

Although the Office of Special Counsel reportedly lacks funds and personnel, whistleblowers who are covered by the WPA appear better off with it than without it.[58] Despite its shortcomings, the need for CIA employees to be able to avail themselves of this resource seems imperative.

That classified matters may be involved if the CIA is included under the WPA is not an insurmountable problem. Federal Bureau of Investigation (FBI) employees, who also require security clearances and handle classified information and counterintelligence activities, are covered under the WPA. In February 1998, in fact, a veteran FBI agent and laboratory chemist reached a $1.16 million settlement from the FBI in exchange for dropping a lawsuit alleging that the FBI had retaliated against him for being a whistleblower and criticizing the FBI laboratory's handling of evidence in several major cases.[59]

The Equal Employment Opportunity Commission (EEOC) provides a working example of a government entity established by federal statute which has been set up to deal with cases involving federal agencies, including those whose employees work in foreign intelligence and counterintelligence. Certain EEOC employees and judges have been designated for CIA cases and problems. They possess the security clearances and the safe storage facilities necessary for handling classified matters.

Similarly, the Office of Special Counsel could obtain security clearances on a selected number of its officials, who could investigate allegations of reprisal and retaliation against CIA employees who report wrongdoing. Obtaining appropriate safes for the storage of classified material, as well as alarms and locks, would not be difficult and likely would be a one-time expenditure.

The alternative—reporting CIA wrongdoing or misconduct to the CIA's Inspector General or the Director—does not protect the whistleblower from retaliation (see Chapter Three, Section B). On the contrary, it could merely serve to assist the CIA in hiding its dirty laundry.

---

blown, agency use of confidentiality restrictions to stifle whistleblowing and broad exemptions from whistleblower protections including exemption of the CIA).

58. *Id.* at 415.

59. Roberto Suro, *Whistle-Blower to Get Documents*, Wash. Post, Mar. 12, 1998, at A13.

G. Conclusion

Combining judicial and legislative remedies might be an effective approach in attempting to bring some balance into the grossly disparate situation that exists between the employee, as the plaintiff, and an intelligence agency or its managers, as the defendant. The burden of proof could be shifted to the intelligence agency, which should be required to meet that burden under the heightened clear and convincing standard. At the same time, the intelligence agency should be made to comply with early and continuing mandatory disclosure requirements. If it delays and obstructs the process, the agency should be sanctioned for failure to participate in good faith discovery under the Federal Rules of Civil Procedure. Before and during litigation, an intelligence agency's attempts to hide behind secrecy could be remedied to a large extent by the courts' use of such means as in camera judicial review, the appointment of a special master, requiring the agency to admit or stipulate to relevant facts which the excluded classified information would tend to prove, finding against the agency on issues to which the excluded classified information relates and striking the testimony of any government witness who is unable to fully and truthfully respond for ostensible reasons of national security. Importantly, security clearances for a CIA plaintiff's lawyer(s) should be requested from and granted by a United States government agency other than the CIA. Lastly, even if the WPA is limited in its effectiveness, the CIA should not be exempt from its reach.

This combinational approach may work best. As an old CIA warrior once advised me, "there are many ways to skin a cat." If you decide to take on an intelligence agency, there is no half way. You must have a strong case and the inner fortitude and commitment to persevere if you are to prevail.

INDEX